Head of Hope

A Resource & Empowerment Guide

FOR

Living & Thriving with
a Traumatic Brain Injury

Jennifer Soames

TBI Survivor and Advocate, Holistic Health Professional

Disclaimer:

This book is intended to be a source of information and inspiration for living with a
traumatic brain injury (TBI). It is in no way a substitute for treatment or care from a
licensed or certified health professional. I bring my own personal experience, research
and professional expertise to this guide and honor each person's experience as unique.
What helps one person may not be what another person needs at that time. Take what
you need from this book and apply it to your own life and circumstances as you see fit.

ISBN-13 (print book) 978-1-7321646-2-8
ISBN-13 (ebook) 978-1-7321646-3-5

Cover design by O'Daniel Designs

Printed by Gorham Printing in the United States of America

Legacy ONE AUTHORS
Kirkland, WA
LegacyOneAuthors.com

DEDICATION

THIS BOOK IS DEDICATED TO YOU, the reader, and all the millions of others in the world who live with a traumatic brain injury. May you grow in knowledge, strength, courage, faith and wisdom for your continued healing journey ahead and live a life of health and happiness.

Also, words cannot express my gratitude to my husband, who has been my greatest rock and supporter throughout this whole adventure. Without you in my life, babe, I would not be the woman I am today or have been able to write this book. You have my heart and love for all eternity.

CONTENTS

INTRODUCTION

From One Survivor to Another

From one traumatic brain injury (TBI) survivor to another, let me first say, "Congratulations!" Why? Because you are a *survivor* and one strong, bad-ass person, in my opinion, who commands a round of applause, tons of respect, and probably a medal of some sort. Not only have you said "yes" to your own empowerment by picking up this book, you have made the commitment to yourself to live your best life possible with a traumatic brain injury. My hope for you is to not just *survive* with a TBI but *thrive* within your own personal experience and in every aspect of your life.

My journey of healing and recovery since my TBI has honestly been a very lonely road at times. Though I have received excellent care from numerous practitioners/professionals and have the support of many friends and family, for which I am so very grateful, no one has been able to guide me on a clear path through my process of healing, adapting and learning to live with the challenges I experience. Many times I have felt lost in the forest without a GPS, compass, or even a trail map, wandering aimlessly trying to find someone or something that can help me.

You are not alone. I want to provide you with information, inspiration and resources of which you may be not be aware. My life with a TBI has taught me more about myself than I probably ever wanted to know, but it has not been without a lot of struggle, frustration, and pure anger and pain. I share my story and write this book so that you, hopefully, will not have to go through what I have been through. No one held my hand, except my husband, and guided me from the beginning on what to do or who to see. I hope that this book acts as a metaphorical hand to guide you in the right direction with as little confusion and frustration as possible.

Though awareness about brain injuries has increased significantly in recent years, mostly due to my country's love of football, there is still a generalized walk-it-off mentality, meaning, "just walk it off and you'll be fine. It's no big deal. Just keep living your life exactly as you have, as if it never happened." This mentality must change. Brain injuries are no laughing matter (except when we laugh at ourselves), or something to be shrugged off. A TBI is a serious, life-altering trauma that can have mild to devastating effects, both immediately and decades after the initial occurrence; physically, emotionally and, I will personally add, spiritually. Come on, world, these are our *brains* we're talking about: command central for our bodies, thoughts, personalities, intellect, creativity, communication and so much more. It is a big deal!

Most of the time, there are no scars, casts or bandages. We live with invisible wounds, affected in ways that the rest of the world just cannot grasp. To everyone else we appear normal and fine on the outside, yet I have often felt neither normal nor fine. Can you relate? The more we start to share our stories and educate others about living with a traumatic brain injury, the more we can start to shift the general mindset away from "walk it off," and instead, toward prevention, clearer guidance on treatment, greater empathy and healing.

So here's to you, my fellow TBI friend, for your courage and strength in the journey so far, and the one that lies ahead. You are not alone. I hope this book leaves you feeling empowered to be your own advocate in your healing process and seeking ways and people to help you move forward and be happy in your life, even with a traumatic brain injury.

PART I

BACKGROUND

What exactly is a traumatic brain injury (TBI)?

Before we can talk about moving forward with life after a traumatic brain injury, we must first have the necessary background information to start on the same page. The general public, and even the health care industry, seems to have a lot of misunderstanding about what constitutes a traumatic brain injury. A TBI is a head injury from blunt trauma to the head or rapid acceleration/deceleration of the brain within the cranium (skull) that disrupts normal brain function. Not all head trauma results in a TBI, and the severity of a TBI ranges from mild to severe, (written in the medical world as mTBI, or sTBI, respectfully). It's important to note that the qualifying terms of mild to severe for a TBI describe solely the amount of physiological damage to the brain, not the severity of symptoms that the person experiences resulting from the injury. Just because it is diagnosed as mild, does not mean it has mild consequences to the person who sustained the injury.

The diagnosis of TBI relies on symptoms reported immediately after trauma to the head. These symptoms include:[1,2]

- Loss of or impaired consciousness, disorientation and confusion at the time of injury

- Amnesia or memory problems for the event itself
- Nausea
- Irritability, anger and/or difficulty regulating emotions
- Headaches
- Poor concentration
- Dizziness
- Loss of consciousness for less than 30 minutes (note: loss of consciousness is not required for TBI diagnosis)

In the most common instances of brain injury, the force of the head colliding with an object, such as the ground, steering wheel, and other hard surfaces, causes the head and brain to move rapidly back and forth, just like whiplash (one author coined the term "brainlash" to describe this).[3] These sudden movements can damage brain cells when the brain bounces around or twists in the cranium, leading to chemical, neurological and functional changes in the brain. Some people may have visible signs of injury to the head at the time of impact, such as cuts or bruises, but for many of us living with a TBI, there are no visible signs of injury. Brain injuries are often caused by a blow or hit to the head but they can also be caused by brain surgery, such as a tumor removal, a stroke, aneurysm, infection like meningitis, or other events that damage the brain. These, however, are called "acquired brain injuries" by the medical community.[4] Whether considered "traumatic" or "acquired" in origin, people with brain injuries experience a lot of the same symptoms and challenges, even if *how* their brains got damaged differs. Now that you have some essential terminology and background, let's clear up some confusion about concussions.

Is a concussion a TBI?

Often the medical community uses the terms concussion and (m)TBI interchangeably, as a concussion is, in fact, considered a mild traumatic brain injury (mTBI). Though these injuries are not often life- threatening, unless there is subdural (internal) bleeding, a concussion is still a very serious injury and not to be taken lightly. So yes, it is.

What are common symptoms of a TBI?

Depending on the severity and the parts of the brain affected, TBI survivors experience varying symptoms, both acutely and chronically after their injury, as listed below.

COGNITIVE

- Brain fog (not being able to think clearly)
- Memory problems, including amnesia for the event itself
- Delayed response to questions
- Difficulty learning new things
- Trouble concentrating or holding a conversation (easily distracted)
- Difficulty with word recall (finding the words one wants to use)
- Slurred speech

PHYSICAL

- Headaches
- Blurred vision or other vision changes
- Dizziness or fainting
- Nausea or vomiting

- Fatigue (mild to severe)
- Sensitivity to light and/or sound
- Ringing in ears (tinnitus)
- Sleep disturbance (difficulty falling or staying asleep)

EMOTIONAL

- Depression
- Anxiety
- Easily irritable or angry
- Personality changes
- More emotional than "normal"
- Inability to control emotions
- More impulsive

Though many of these symptoms appear immediately, some, like depression, can take months or even years to appear.[5,6] Some of these symptoms can last for days, weeks, or the rest of one's life. This all depends on a multitude of variables.

How common are TBIs?

A study published in 2013 of reported TBI visits to emergency rooms, hospitals and TBI-related deaths in the United States[7] indicated there were approximately 2.8 million TBI-related emergency room visits, hospitalizations, and deaths (combined) per year. "This consisted of approximately 2.5 million TBI-related emergency room visits, approximately 282,000 TBI-related hospitalizations, and approximately 56,000 TBI-related deaths. TBIs were diagnosed in nearly 2.8 million (1.9%) of the approximately 149 million total injury- and non-injury-related [ER visits, hospitalization and deaths] that occurred in the United States during 2013."[7]

The study showed that the causes of TBI were, in greatest to least: falls, being struck by or against an object, and motor vehicle accidents. Over the course of the six-year study, occurrence of reported TBIs increased overall. The study showed that males accounted for more TBIs than women. Though the occurrence of TBI-related hospitalizations due to motor vehicle accidents decreased during the study, the occurrence of fall-related TBI hospitalizations of persons over 75 years increased. So much of our recent focus in TBI prevention has been on athletes, particularly youth. The numbers from this study, however, show that emphasis on fall prevention in older persons (aged 75 or older) could, in fact, significantly reduce the number of TBIs that occur every year.

At the time of this writing, the United States (US) has approximately 325 million people.[8] That means if there are 2.8 million reported TBIs annually, then .86% of the US population incurs a TBI every year: just under 1%. Note that the numbers reported by the study referenced above are of *reported* TBIs. Because there is a generalized "walk it off" mentality around a bump or blow to the head, many people do not seek medical treatment, particularly in emergency rooms and hospitals following head trauma. It's likely that the actual number of people who acquire a traumatic brain injury every year is substantially higher.

To put it in perspective of another devastating health challenge, an estimated 1.7 million new cases of cancer are diagnosed in the United States each year.[9] *There are almost twice as many TBIs than cancer diagnoses annually in the US* (1.75:1, respectively, if you do the math). Yikes! So much attention is given to cancer, and rightfully so. But where is the attention and focus on prevention and effective treatment of traumatic brain injuries when they affect almost twice as many people as cancer? We're getting there, but not fast enough for all the people struggling, not knowing what to do or who to see, or how to truly live with a TBI.

Now that we've defined a TBI and its causes and symptoms, let's make our first moves toward understanding, healing and living. Moving forward begins with sharing our story. So here is mine.

My Story: How did this happen?

It was Friday, November 22, 2013, the Friday before Thanksgiving. I drove just over an hour to my friend and trainer's barn for a dressage (a style of English riding) lesson. I've been a horse enthusiast and equestrian since I was a girl and even spent my teenage years as an elite athlete in the sport of vaulting (gymnastics on horseback). It would be an understatement to say that I've been on horses a lot and have loved and continue to love every minute with and on a horse.

For some reason I cannot remember, the horse I usually rode wasn't available that day. So I rode a horse I knew by name but had never ridden. Her name was Glory. Glory didn't like adult riders. She liked kids, mostly because she could get away with more shenanigans and work less if kids were riding her. Seeing as how I'm only 5′1″ tall, to Glory I probably appeared a large child. When I asked her, in our lesson, to do some challenging moves, it was clear she was not happy about it. We worked through our disagreements and she reluctantly made the effort to do what I asked. Then, as we were trotting in a large circle, she spooked. Glory jumped completely sideways to the right but no matter my skills as a rider, I could not stay on. I came off to the left, twisting and landing on my back and hitting the back of my head on the arena ground. Hard. Thankfully, I always ride with a helmet. No matter how good a rider I think I am, I don't take chances.

I lay there on my back on the ground and heard my trainer yell across the arena, "Don't move!" I lay there, remaining still, but though I was conscious, I couldn't see. Whether it was only for a couple seconds or a minute, I don't know. I have no idea how long I couldn't see. Time is skewed and impossible to measure in moments like that. It was the weirdest thing to not be able to see, even with my eyes open. Nothing. Just dark.

My trainer ran over to my side to make sure I was okay. My vision returned, and though very shaken up, once I could see again and realized that I had no broken bones, I did the only rational thing that any rider does in these situations: I got back on Glory. To be honest, doing so was a bit scary. I sat on the horse shaking and crying as the gravity of the situation hit me.

Shaking and crying is a normal way to discharge trauma, and it was all I could do for a couple minutes before I continued with my lesson. I rode for another 15 minutes, just to finish on a good note. Yes, Glory was extremely sorry for the incident. That was clear. It's hard to describe to non-horse people, but just trust me on this: her demeanor changed right away. Once I came off, this time voluntarily, I unsaddled Glory, put her back in her pasture and spent a little time talking with my trainer friend. Though I had a really bad headache, I thought I was fine. It wasn't until I started on my long drive home that I realized something was truly wrong. I got increasingly and unusually tired.

"Shit!" I thought to myself, "I have a concussion." Though I had never had a concussion before, despite being involved with horses from an early age, I had written a paper many years earlier on the high incidence of concussions in those who participate in equine activities. Intuitively, I just knew I was one of those sobering statistics. I made it safely home to ice and rest. Little did I know that from that point on, I would begin a life-changing journey. It kicked off with the worst night of my life thus far, and I really do hope, ever, with the worst pain in my head I could possibly imagine.

I woke up bawling in pain. I could not lie flat with my head in line with my heart. The pressure and throbbing in my head was too much to bear, so I sat in bed, crying. My dear husband frantically searched the internet to find out which over-the-counter pain killer he could give me that was not a blood thinner (potentially dislodging a clot, if one existed). I finally got the pain under control enough that I could sleep for a few hours.

Thankfully, being a holistic health professional, before I even drove away from the barn that fateful afternoon I called my friend and colleague, Nancy, a very experienced and skilled CranioSacral practitioner. She said she could see me that evening, but I opted to wait till the next morning. I didn't want to go anywhere else but home.

Having had a little sleep, my husband drove me to see Nancy on Saturday morning. I entered my chiropractor's office, where she had her practice, looking and feeling like death. It may sound like an exaggeration, but that's how I felt. After a gentle chiropractic adjustment, I had my session with Nancy. Because I had already known Nancy for a couple of years at that point and highly respected her both as a professional and a friend, I, admittedly reluctantly, agreed to go to the emergency room (ER) to get a CT scan of my head to make sure I didn't have a subdural hematoma (internal bleeding in my brain). Why I didn't think of this on Friday afternoon, I don't know. Goes to show how much I valued my own brain and life at the time. Seriously. I decided to get the CT scan because Nancy told me to, and not because I thought it was truly necessary. I was too worried about the financial cost, even with the good health insurance we had. But reluctantly, I went. Thankfully, the CT scan came out "clean," not revealing any internal bleeding. The ER staff examined me, gave me prescription-strength pain killers and sent me on my way with a two-page handout basically saying to take it easy, and told me to follow up with my primary physician in a couple of weeks.

In truth, once the CT scan had been reviewed, the ER doc came in and verbatim said, "Congratulations! You're concussed!" When I reflect on that moment and those words, you have no idea how many mixed emotions I feel now.

With the attitude projected by the ER staff of, "it's no big deal, you'll be just fine and in no time," my husband and I set off for a quick errand, and then home. Of course, I was in no condition to drive since my brain could and would not think, even if I wanted it to. Just about three and a half miles short of being home, we approached an intersection with a traffic light. It was green for us, so of course my husband kept moving forward through the intersection. But we didn't make it through the intersection. A woman in the left turn lane from the opposite direction failed to yield to our right of way and turned left directly in front of us. My husband did his best to avoid hitting her, but physics was not in our favor. We hit the back right end of her car with the front passenger side of our car. Yeah, *my* side. We pulled over into the parking lot of the market next to us to assess the damage of machines and humans alike and exchange insurance information. I couldn't open my door. The impact had damaged my side enough that the only way out was climbing out the driver's side door. I chose to let my husband handle it, though, as I was too angry and didn't think I could resist screaming at the lady who caused the accident. Just like the horse, the driver, too, was very sorry.

To say I was pissed off would be an understatement, as my vehicle was only 13 months old and the only car I've ever bought brand new. That came to my mind first. It was only then that I realized that my neck pain was *extremely* bad, despite being on prescription pain killers from the hospital, which were very much still in effect. The front of my neck (sternocleido-mastoids specifically) was painful and my head was throbbing again (it had stopped throbbing after my CranioSacral therapy session if I kept my head above my heart). Though I did not hit my head on the frame of the car or the windshield, in any whiplash event the head gets thrown forward and then gets snapped back and hits the headrest of the seat. My head was no exception to this. My poor brain got banged around in my skull some more. Thankfully, my husband and the other woman were both unharmed.

We waited for over an hour for State Patrol to finally show up. Thankfully, the woman claimed full responsibility for the accident, as that was the truth of the situation. Two head traumas in approximately 25 hours. Seriously, what are the odds? I guessed I rolled my dice well on that one!

First thing on Monday morning I called my attorney and said, "I have another one for you." Almost exactly a year prior, we had been in a very bad car accident on the freeway in which I was also a passenger, being in the middle of a three-car pileup and the recipient of two highway speed impacts, one at each end, within seconds of each other. I sustained many injuries in that accident and had literally ended accident-related treatment about six weeks prior to that fateful weekend in November.

I began to tell my attorney about the damage to the car and she was the one to stop me and ask, "But, how are *you?*" I disclosed the fall from the horse on Friday and how I had been feeling since the car accident on Saturday. We both knew this was going to be a very tricky and complicated case because these two incidents were only one day apart. I was more concerned with getting my car fixed and compensated for its devaluation, since it now had an accident on its record. Four thousand dollars in repairs to my car later, I started to really experience the seriousness and pain of what had happened to *me*.

What Doctors Never Told Me

When I left the ER from getting the CT scan, I was given a two-page handout on care for a concussion. I no longer have it, so I cannot remember exactly what it said other than basically to take it easy, rest a lot, don't use your brain much, and follow up with your primary physician in two weeks.

With my brain in a complete fog and experiencing intense pain if I bent down to pick something up, mostly out of habit, when my head went below my heart, I had neck and back pain that surfaced within a day or two of the car accident. I was feeling exhausted and just "off," so I did my best to rest. Being self-employed, however, and needing both my husband's and my incomes, I took the few clients I had that week, as scheduled. Nope, I didn't cancel any of them. Being the week of Thanksgiving, it was a short work week anyway, and fairly slow with client appointments. My head hurt. Even my eyes hurt. It hurt to look left and right, which may sound strange, but it was true. I had intense sensitivity to light and sound.

I continued to see my chiropractor and receive CranioSacral therapy from Nancy. I was fortunate enough to even have an appointment that Wednesday, the day before Thanksgiving, with my Neurolink practitioner (I'll dive into these modalities later), which reduced my eye pain by at least 90% in 30 minutes. No joke.

On Thanksgiving, we went down to my sister-in-law's house which just happened to be just miles from the barn where I had ridden the Friday before. I was barely able to stay awake after a few hours, and not from an abundance of turkey. We had to leave early. Thankfully, the family was sympathetic and could likely tell I wasn't doing well by the time we left.

My follow-up visit to my primary physician was fairly insignificant from what I can remember. It consisted of checking in from the fall and the car accident, an exam and an agreement to continue with chiropractic care, CranioSacral therapy and other bodywork (hands-on therapies) as needed. As the weeks progressed and the holidays came and went, I cautiously eased my way back into going to the gym and yoga and avoided exercises or postures that brought my head down below my heart, since this still caused my head to throb painfully. Using the leg press machine or doing squats at the gym also caused my head to throb, so I stopped doing those exercises and took it very easy in my workouts for quite some time. The brain fog slowly started to clear. I pretty much continued with life as usual. It was my impression that I would be fine in a couple of weeks, given the nonchalant attitude of the ER staff and the simple two-page handout.

By mid-January I knew I wasn't "right." Though my sleep patterns had been affected by my hormone cycle for a while, particularly after the first car accident in 2012, with disrupted sleep as I got closer to menstruation, I noticed that I was having disrupted sleep *every* night, regardless of my hormones. Prior to the injuries in November 2013, thanks to working with my doctor, my hormones had been improving. But by mid-to-late January, I really knew something had gone terribly wrong, not to mention the fact that I was definitely more irritable and snappy than usual (just ask my husband), and my balance wasn't as good as it had been previous to the concussion. Having grown up a ballerina and vaulter, my balance had always been good. Though it was still considered excellent compared to the average Joe, I could tell my balance wasn't good for *me*. I had a really hard time doing balancing postures in yoga that I'd done for years without much wavering.

The other chiropractor I saw on occasion (I saw two who practiced completely different techniques) recommended a local functional neurologist of whom she had heard who works specifically with people with brain injuries. I knew I had to do something. The insomnia was becoming unbearable. Eventually, I contacted the neurologist and made an appointment. Though I will get into the explanation and details of functional neurology later, I will say that my work with this neurologist was incredibly helpful. Over the next few months, sometimes working with him daily for weeks at a time, I regained control over my emotions, my balance returned to what is normal for me, and my cognitive functions improved significantly. When people ask me, "What did you actually *do* with your neurologist?" they are in for a bit of a surprise.

My functional neurologist began our course of treatment by looking at my eyes and eye movement. I wore a special, goggle-like apparatus on my head that was connected to one of his many computer screens. He had me do certain tasks, movements and more wearing these googles. Depending on what we were doing, and how he saw my eyes respond, he could tell how parts of my brain were functioning (or not). Though I could never fully follow all of what and why we did the things we did, despite being an educated licensed health professional myself, it made sense enough.

We did a lot of brain games, particularly using a website called Lumosity,[10,] but we upped the brain game challenges significantly. Because of my inability to sleep, one of his goals in our work together was to physically and mentally exhaust me to discharge the excess, stressed-out energy of being in a constant fight or flight state, with the intention of wearing me out so much that I would sleep. While playing Lumosity brain games, I would have to do physical challenges, like push-ups while walking sideways in a push-up ("plank") position and verbally answering math questions as they popped up faster and faster on the tablet screen he held in front of me as I moved. We even brought my treatments onto an indoor soccer field. My functional neurologist had me running complex drills, and jumping over small hurdles while saying the alphabet, every other letter starting with B, and then doing it again, but in reverse, starting with Z. I could go on with a multitude of examples of the seemingly crazy things that comprised my treatments, but I think you get the idea. It may seem crazy, but boy did he know his stuff!

Because of my overly-heightened fight or flight (sympathetic nervous system) state and other details I shared with him, my neurologist also diagnosed me with PTSD, primarily from the multiple car accidents within a year's time. So now I had a TBI *and* PTSD. Great. Just great. "This wasn't supposed to happen to *me*!" I thought. But guess what? It did, and it was my reality. I went to counseling. Therapy helped with some of the PTSD issues I was having, as well as the immediate challenges I experienced as I began this healing process. It was not an easy or enjoyable time in my life, I admit, but damn it, I was determined to get back to the way I used to be before my TBI.

My sleep? Well, it did improve, due in part to taking diphenhydramine (the active ingredient in Benadryl) every night, which I later learned when I researched online (but can't locate the specific site now), maybe wasn't the best idea right after a concussion. I tried just about every holistic remedy, herb and supplement out there, to no avail. This isn't to say they didn't work. Rather, they weren't what I needed at that point in time. I slept a bit better, but never felt rested. I often woke up for a few hours at night, tossed and turned, and eventually fell back asleep right around the time I used to get up prior to my TBI.

Before my TBI I was known as a morning person. Everyone knew me to get up early and be at the gym or the yoga studio by 5:30-6:00 a.m. I prided myself on it. In a very short amount of time, that part of my identity got rewritten. I was no longer a morning person. Yoga classes at 6:00 a.m. were not happening for me anymore, especially when I'd lie awake between 1:00-4:00 a.m., and maybe fall back asleep by 5:00 a.m. for a few more hours. It was very hard to function on days when preceding nights included only a few hours of sleep. I had no trouble falling asleep at all. It was just the staying asleep part that was killing me. Insomnia is literally torture. Now I fully understand why it is used as such. At times during those first few months post TBI, it was so bad that I really wanted to kill myself. The thought of endless rest was so tempting. Rest was all I wanted. It wasn't that I thought I had nothing to live for, or that I truly had any intention of on acting on these thoughts (known in psychology as passive suicidal ideation). Rather, I just couldn't take the lack of sleep anymore! I know it scared my husband one night, in the wee hours of the morning, as I lay there crying and telling him I just wanted it all to end. He was afraid of coming home to a dead wife. I promised him in every way I knew how that I was not going to act on these disturbing thoughts. It was the chronic lack of sleep talking.

By the end of May 2014, I wrapped up my treatment with my functional neurologist, as he and I both felt I was really doing quite well. I was, in many ways. It was a relief to reduce the number of medical appointments I had every week, and finally take a much-needed vacation to Hawaii with my husband for our anniversary. By the end of June, though, things started to change for the worse. Again.

Even though my sleep was doing a bit better and overall I was feeling more like myself again, by June I noticed that I was having a REALLY hard time getting out of bed in the morning. Devoid of energy, it could take me anywhere from 30 minutes to two hours to get out of bed. Again, something wasn't right. I went back to my primary physician. We did some blood work and it showed that my thyroid levels were low, which surprised me for being only 30 and in generally good health. We agreed to try some thyroid medication to boost it, and hence, my energy. After a few months, things didn't seem to improve, even though my bloodwork came back with normal thyroid levels, thanks to the medication. Over the years of my experience and research since, it's evident that thyroid dysfunction is not uncommon in people post TBI, which we'll get into more in a bit.[11,12,13]

By the end of October and early November 2014, nearing the first anniversary of my TBI, I was not doing well. I was emotional, exhausted, still not sleeping great and unhappy. I was diagnosed with clinical depression and reluctantly started on Prozac. "Seriously", I thought, "this *cannot* be happening to me! As a holistic health professional, I'm supposed to be the epitome of health, and not taking pharmaceuticals!" Regardless of my then ideas of how I was supposed to be and appear to the world, this was, in fact, happening.

Once I began researching TBIs and depression, it was evident that there is a huge connection, and one that, in my opinion, is not being shared enough with both TBI survivors and the general public. I came across research articles going back to the Vietnam War era linking the two.[14] None of my practitioners said, "Let me know if you develop any of these symptoms [of depression]." Of course, it would not have been a good idea to have any of my doctors or health care team say, "You'll likely end up with depression in the first year," which many studies indicate is common,[6] because it's not a good idea to plant those seeds in a patient or client's mind. It often creates needless anxiety and the person ends up with the condition that was suggested, bringing the prophecy to fruition. Let me make it clear that I do not blame any of my providers for negligence regarding this depression diagnosis. It just blindsided me. If I had known, though, to be on the lookout for and report some of the symptoms (even without giving it the name, "depression"), I might have sought treatment sooner. This is why I'm sharing this with you and other people I meet who have recently incurred a TBI: so you can be aware and seek treatment right away if symptoms appear.

"So much for the two-page handout I received at the ER," I thought. Maybe some people return to normal after two weeks of rest. If they really *are* back to their normal, I envy them. However, I am very sensitive, and also very in tune with my body to know when something is off, which is one of the gifts and curses of doing the work I do professionally. Taking it easy had clearly not been enough, and yet no one prepared me for this journey that I had begun. It was one that would prove to be the most difficult, educational, and rewarding of my life so far.

In August 2015, after being on a wait-list for many months, I finally got in for an appointment with a highly recommended TBI specialist at a local hospital. I particularly wanted his thoughts and professional insights regarding my situation of having two impacts to my head within about 25 hours. He listened intently and patiently as I shared my story. We talked, he answered the list of questions I brought with me, performed a physical exam and diagnosed me with post-concussion syndrome (PCS).

Post-concussion syndrome describes a condition in which a TBI survivor continues to experience concussion symptoms for months or years after the initial injury. These include:[15, 16]

COGNITIVE

- Memory problems
- Problems with executive functioning (which control behavior)
- Difficulty learning new things
- Trouble concentrating or focusing
- Difficulty with problem solving

PHYSICAL

- Headaches
- Blurred vision or other vision changes

- Dizziness

- Fatigue (mild to severe)

- Sensitivity to light and/or sound

- Sleep disturbance (difficulty falling or staying asleep)

EMOTIONAL

- Depression

- Anxiety

- Easily irritable or angry

- Personality changes

- More emotional than "normal"

- Inability to control emotions

- More impulsive

Looks exactly like the list of symptoms following a concussion from earlier in this book, doesn't it? Because it is. These symptoms just linger. Why? There are numerous variables. Women are more likely to experience them than men. At least women tend to seek treatment more than men, which could be the reason for the statistic. Older people are more likely to experience PCS as well. If there is history of concussion, or double impact (sounds familiar), history of mood disorders (depression, anxiety, and more), the chances increase.[16] Excessive physical or mental activity can exacerbate these symptoms, but they can also occur at rest. PCS can be minor to debilitating, causing some to make big changes that affect their family, career and social life. For me, it has deeply impacted my social and professional life. How I've managed to maintain and grow a professional practice blows my mind at times. Unfortunately, my TBI specialist couldn't really speak to the impact of the car accident that occurred on the way home from the ER. He did say, however, that the severe car accident in which I was also passenger in 2012 likely was a huge factor in developing PCS, since I had experienced physical and psychological trauma only a year prior to my TBI.

By the time I saw the TBI specialist, I had been experiencing PCS for more than two and a half years. Some websites I searched indicated that PCS often lasts for just a few months, or even a year. Well, I'm living proof that it can last much longer than that. I still experience PCS symptoms years later. Every person is different, and every TBI survivor has their own unique experience. This is mine. Is there more I had to find out for myself? You better believe it! It doesn't end there, so keep reading.

Closure

Finally, in March 2017, my car accident settlements came through. Because I had entered into another legal case following the car accident that occurred on the way home from the ER, I basically had a gag rule for over three years. Of course, I could say I had a traumatic brain injury, but I could not go into the details or share photos of the car or any other information on social media or with anyone who didn't need to know. As such, per my attorney's strong recommendation, I could lurk in TBI support groups on Facebook, but I couldn't ever post or comment. I was so afraid of my Facebook account being subpoenaed that I wouldn't even talk about the details of anything related to these incidents in Facebook Messenger or any other online format where my identity was or could be revealed. I felt so incredibly alone, even though I knew there were online communities of people who fully understood. Though I know I could have found a regionally local TBI support group to join in person, I didn't have the energy. The thought of driving around the greater Seattle metro area (we have some of the worst traffic in the nation) was exhausting, and I just couldn't bring myself to do it, especially when I was in the full throes of depression.

When I later gave talks to women's groups on self-care (something about which I am very passionate personally and professionally), I would share my story, keeping it broad and general and would specifically ask attendees to not record or post anything on social media or the internet about my story, except their "aha" moments and takeaways from the rest of the presentation. This forced silence was agonizing for me and really felt like an imaginary ball and chain strapped to my leg, holding me back and keeping me from really moving on with my life. I knew, and even my TBI specialist agreed, that when there are legal cases associated with injuries and traumas, the moment they close, healing really begins.

From November 2013, I waited. And waited. And waited. Due to the complexities of my case, and because of how soon this second car accident occurred after the one a year prior, both auto accident cases got brought together. Honestly, I still don't know how all the legal stuff worked, but I trusted my attorney. I had too many other things to tend to, including my own care (I'll go into navigating the whole legal process later).

After waiting four years and four months, I got an email from my attorney to say that the first accident case (December 2012) was finally closed and I could come pick up my settlement check. I was elated and overjoyed! Then, just four days later, I received another email. After three years, four months and five days (not like I was counting), the second one was closed, and I could pick up another check. I started crying in disbelief and relief. It was finally over. It was surreal. In less than a week, it all came to an end. Closure at last! Silence had been so ingrained in me that I even caught myself messaging a friend of mine on Facebook, only to erase my initial message and replace it instead with the comment that I would call her with good news. I had to laugh at myself shortly after I wrote that, because it didn't matter anymore. I was free. No more silence or gag rule. Yes, the financial compensation was a huge relief since I had incurred so much debt with medical bills, coupled with my decreased ability to work, but truly, knowing that this long-lasting battle was finally over brought me the greatest relief. It had taken a huge emotional toll.

Once the metaphorical ball and chain of these legal cases had been removed from my life, I really felt free, and that I could truly move forward with my life and healing. I never realized the weight associated with closure. It felt like 1000 lbs. got lifted off me!

What happens, though, when there is no closure?

I was fortunate to obtain some closure through these legal cases, but there is no closure in the reality that I, you, or others living with a TBI face daily. Instead, the focus shifts away from closure and toward healing, accepting, adapting, and learning not just how to live, but *thrive*, with a chronic condition. The future, along with *what* will change, and *if* things will change, is uncertain. My hope, though, is to share my story not for sake of sympathy (I have had way too much of that), but instead to inspire and be a resource to others. My silence is broken, and it's my hope that my voice, whether spoken or written, will be used to help you heal, accept, adapt, live and thrive in your best life, no matter what.

Is the lack closure in your own life weighing you down? If so, how is it showing up? Is there a way to find closure in your own situation? If not, then how can you move forward? Surrounding yourself with a skilled and empathetic healthcare team is an essential part of moving forward. Establishing that team can be one of the greatest challenges.

Lessons Learned from Selecting My Healthcare Team

Life continued into the second and third year post-TBI, as I adapted to and worked on accepting a new version of Me, which was and continues to be a journey in and of itself. I continued with medications, yoga, coaching, counseling and self-care. I added and fired doctors from my team. The journey made me realize the incredible need for better communication, understanding and education among healthcare professionals and with their TBI patients. When I went to one doctor in hopes of getting more answers and solutions for my chronic fatigue, the doctor thought I had Lyme disease. I did expensive blood tests that came back inconclusive (which most do), though I've never knowingly been bitten by a tick in my life. I've lived in the Pacific Northwest nearly all my life, and we generally do not have ticks here in Western Washington, even though that is starting to change in certain areas. Being so emotionally fragile in my depressed state, I had a total meltdown when the doctor told me she thought I had Lyme disease. I did not have the ability to cope with that possibility on top of everything else.

In fact, no, I did and do not have Lyme disease, as later tests showed that is not the reason for my chronic fatigue (more on that soon). She gave it her best educated guess, but it wasn't right, so I took her off my team.

I had another doctor, the one who diagnosed me with depression, whom I also fired. When I expressed concern about the interactions of fluoxetine (Prozac) and Trazodone (which I took to help me sleep) per my conversation with a pharmacist and the warning about taking the two together in the information sheet that comes with your medication, I took her response as defensive and without regard to my concerns. Whether or not it was defensive, it was my interpretation at the time. One thing I've learned both as a patient and a health professional, is the need and desire for people to be heard by their practitioners. I did not feel heard and decided to discontinue seeing this doctor. I strongly advocate for finding the right practitioner(s) at the right time. These practitioners, whether they are allopathic (Western) or holistic, should, in my opinion, do the following:

1. Listen

2. Explain the facts while being open to the fact that people respond differently to each approach

3. Present findings in a clear, concise way with consideration for their client/patient's emotional state

4. Be willing to address questions and concerns without an inflated ego

5. Not be patronizing or condescending

All this, and the willingness and ability for practitioners to work together as needed for the sake of their clients and patients, are some of my core values when seeking my professional health care team.

Many patients don't feel like it's okay to question their doctors and their recommendations. It is absolutely okay to ask questions, and you *should*. Don't be afraid to ask, "Why?" After all, this is YOU we are talking about: your body, your experience and your care. You have every right to ask questions. I encourage you to get as much information as you can before you make a decision on a course of treatment, medication, or care. Ask about the risks *and* benefits. Ask about the side effects of a medication and coming off a medication *before* you begin taking it. I learned this the hard way when I eventually came off Prozac. Whew, that was a roller coaster and a challenging process! I wish I would have asked about the side effects of coming off it before I started. It would not have changed my decision to take the medication, but it would have been nice to have full disclosure before I committed to it.

Become your own advocate. Do the research yourself or have someone help you so that you can have educated discussions with your health care team while honoring their expertise and professional experience. They do know a lot, but they also don't know everything (Believe me, I know this first hand in my own professional practice). They are just as human as you and me. Though we may not always want to hear what they have to say, especially if the news isn't what we were hoping, I encourage you to keep an open mind and heart as you continue on your own journey and find practitioners who will support you in your physical, emotional and spiritual health. Sometimes it takes trial and error to find the right members of your team. It's okay to respectfully let your practitioners know what you want and what you do not want when it comes to your care. It is okay to ask questions. Just get all the information before you decide how you want to proceed so that you feel confident about and supported in the direction you're headed.

Finally: Answers

Despite the challenges I faced with cognitive processing, memory, word recall, blood pressure (varied between getting light-headed and having throbbing pressure in my head), depressive episodes, imbalanced hormones, chronic fatigue, some sleep disturbances and being medicated, life actually moved along pretty well. I continued with treatments and medication but reduced my frequency of treatments. I was so tired of appointments: all the driving, energy and time. Plus, I acquired significant debt from medical bills, coupled with my reduced ability to work. Despite the hardship, I was determined to keep moving forward with my life and purpose. In 2016 I flew across the country to study and complete my yoga teacher certification. This was a huge accomplishment for me and a big milestone in moving forward with my life and professional goals. Life was starting to look up.

As time moves on, my quality of life continues to improve. I keep learning more about the repercussions of my injuries and what it takes to heal. In 2017 I decided I wanted additional, objective data on my brain function. It had been two and half years since I did any objective tests with my functional neurologist, and I decided to follow through with a recommendation a friend of mine (also a TBI survivor) made for a neuropsychologist. At that point, I didn't know which of my behaviors and habits I could legitimately blame on the TBI, and which were just my habits and behaviors. After about five hours of rigorous brain challenges and tests, the evaluation was complete. I was exhausted and brain dead. I returned for the results a couple weeks later. From the perspective of a neuropsychologist, my brain looked pretty good. Those short-term memory problems I thought I had? Well, it looks more like I have trouble getting new information *into* my brain in the first place. Once information does sink in, I have the physiological capacity to remember it, under controlled conditions. It just takes me more repetitions to hook, line, and sink 'er into my noggin. So, when I can't remember things, like people's names that I just met, it's not necessarily that I don't have the capability to remember. Rather, the information didn't go in in the first place. It still appears to the outside world and to me like a memory problem, even though the actual mechanism is different.

From my evaluation, I also learned that I have a really hard time with puzzle tasks. Not jigsaw puzzles, but recognizing complex patterns, especially in a sequence. Hard to say if this was a challenge of mine before the TBI or not, but it was interesting information nonetheless. All the other functions tested appeared within normal range, per the standards and statistics the industry has for these tests. This is, of course, excellent news, though it doesn't change the fact that I still struggle with remembering things, have trouble finding the words I want to say in my mental dictionary, slower mental processing times than pre-TBI, and it takes me a little longer to get things done. It also doesn't account for my chronic fatigue or hormone imbalances.

The neuropsychologist acknowledged that all this data about my brain did not account for how I have to navigate in the real world, where there are distractions, to-do lists, deadlines, and so much more. These tests were done in a controlled setting to see if my brain could carry out the empirical tasks related to memory, problem solving, etc. It was a relief to know that, from a neuropsychological view, my brain is working quite well. I still felt exhausted and frustrated. My neuropsychologist said, "Normally I would recommend all the things you're doing, but you're already doing them." Though she didn't have a lot to offer in way of continued treatment with her, she referred me to a sleep specialist and a neuroendocrinologist to try to help get to the root cause of my sleep and hormonal challenges.

Because my sleep had been chronically disrupted and unrestful since my TBI, seeing a sleep specialist had been recommended to me numerous times. I knew a lot about and practiced good sleep hygiene,[17] as it's called, so I was very reluctant to see a sleep specialist or undergo a sleep study, thinking there wasn't much they could offer me. As the founder of an association of health professionals in my area that I started in 2012, I organized our annual symposium in 2014 on the topic of sleep. It wasn't my idea, but that of my members, and I was very excited to host it. I learned a lot about sleep hygiene and ever since have practiced good sleep hygiene, like limiting caffeine intake and avoiding it after 12 p.m., not using electronics or exercising immediately before bed, getting up and going out to the couch if I couldn't sleep (and then going back to bed when I was about to nod off again), making sure my room was dark and cool, and more.[15] Despite my diligence, I still couldn't stay asleep for more than a handful of hours most nights.

I admit I was a bit cocky, a know-it-all, and resisted the recommendation for a sleep specialist every time. From talking with people who had been to a sleep specialist, it seemed that all the specialists ever tested for is sleep apnea. I do not have sleep apnea. I breathe at night and breathe through my nose. I've even had my husband creepily watch me while I sleep to make sure of this. I did not want to be hooked up to machines and watched by a stranger while I slept. This would, I knew, ensure that I would <u>not</u> sleep! Thankfully, my primary physician, along with my neuropsychologist, referred me to an excellent sleep specialist who she knew would not automatically send me for a sleep study to test for sleep apnea. Though reluctant and skeptical, I finally went. When I recapped my history to the sleep specialist, he said, "Your case is very complicated." Yes, it is. "Duh," I thought. He thought for a minute and then gave me his recommendations. He did not think a sleep study was indicated (whew), but he did think I needed to shift my sleep pattern so that I would start sleeping through the night. With this repeatable pattern of waking up in the wee hours of the morning, he said, it was like being chronically jet lagged. That, indeed, is how I often felt: jet lagged. Though this disrupted sleep really began due to the TBI, he thought that other factors were perpetuating it. But he didn't give specifics. I was to immediately start staying up later, like 11:00 p.m.-12:00 a.m. if possible, and then set an alarm to get up at 6:00 a.m. I had typically been getting, on average, about six hours of actual sleep per night, but with a few hours here and there of going out to the couch then back to bed, I could spend up to 10 hours in bed, but not actually asleep for that amount of time. His strategy was supposed to help reset my circadian rhythm so that I would get six hours of consecutive sleep per night, and eventually add more.

At first I thought, "Really? Yeah right this is going to help. I won't even be able to stay awake till 11:00 p.m. or midnight I'm so tired!" The sleep specialist assured me that it wasn't forever. He said that I could very slowly, as in 10-minute increments, go to bed earlier and earlier until I found the sweet spot of when my body wanted to go to sleep. He also said that I should still get up at the same time every morning, no matter what.

That night I stayed up, reading a book, until about 11:00 p.m., barely able to stay awake and not happy about staying up late. I've never been a night owl. I honestly can't remember how the first two nights went, but I remember within just four nights, I was sleeping through the night for the first time in years. No matter how crazy it had initially sounded to me, the plan worked. Though I still take a pharmaceutical and supplements to help me sleep, thanks to retraining my sleep pattern, I'm sleeping through the night a lot more often. It's not perfect, as there are times when my sleep has been disrupted for various reasons, but the improvement is remarkable. Who knew? Apparently, the sleep specialist did, and I have since checked my ego. Thankfully my body found the sweet spot time it likes to go to bed, which varies depending on how tired I am, but I am consistently going to bed and waking up around the same times every day. It's amazing how a good night's sleep makes life so much better all around, particularly my mood! At some point I plan to come off medication if my body will sleep without it. After experiencing the horrible side effects of coming off Prozac for depression after the third year into my healing process, I have not been in a rush to wean off this medication. In time, though, I hope it will happen. In the meantime, I'm enjoying sleeping!

After seeing the sleep specialist, one question remained: why do I feel chronically fatigued, to the point of debilitation? The answer revealed itself just days later.

Life Lessons from My Pituitary

Despite doing a lot of different things to help, my hormones had been imbalanced ever since my injuries, with only mild improvement. So, I was willing to see the neuroendocrinologist recommended by both my neuropsychologist and primary physician to get even more objective data. Four days after I saw the sleep specialist I got hooked up to an IV and had blood drawn at regular increments for a cortisol stimulating test. After taking baseline blood samples, the technician injected me with a drug to stimulate my adrenals (but not enough to make me feel any kind of symptoms, thankfully), and then took more blood about 30 minutes later.

When I saw the neuroendocrinologist a couple of hours later, some of the data was back, and it indicated that my adrenals are not producing enough cortisol. Cortisol is the hormone getting a lot of bad rap these days. It is the stress hormone that most people are trying to decrease due to all the problems it can cause when in excess. But, just as with anything in the human body, too little is also a problem.

As he looked at the results, the neuroendocrinologist said something I didn't expect to hear. He said, "Your adrenals can't produce enough cortisol, likely due to pituitary and hypothalamic damage." Though this isn't the news most people want to hear, it was almost music to my ears. For years I'd known intuitively that my pituitary was damaged in my accidents. I knew of only one pituitary endocrinologist in another state who believed that head trauma often damages the pituitary gland. Though I knew this intuitively about my own body, this was the first time a local, reputable, respected neuroendocrinologist backed it up. It was a bit of a relief to hear someone other than myself say that this was one of my problems.

If you're not an anatomy and body nerd like me (after all, it is what I do professionally), allow me to give you some basic and essential information on the pituitary.

The pituitary gland is the master gland of your hormones. It is located roughly just behind the bridge of your nose and is only about the size of a pea. Yeah, it's small. But what's tiny can also be mighty. The posterior, or back portion, of the pituitary gland is attached to the hypothalamus, another brain structure located right above the pituitary.

The tiny pituitary secretes the following hormones:[18]

ANTERIOR PITUITARY:

- Adrenocorticotrophic hormone (ACTH)
- Thyroid-stimulating hormone (TSH)
- Luteinising hormone (LH)
- Follicle-stimulating hormone (FSH)
- Prolactin (PRL)
- Growth hormone (GH)
- Melanocyte-stimulating hormone (MSH)

POSTERIOR PITUITARY:

- Anti-diuretic hormone (ADH)
- Oxytocin

Both men and women have the above hormones, but in different amounts. Based on the list above, there is a lot riding on the health and function of this pea-sized gland. The hypothalamus is a bit larger than the pituitary: the size of an almond. The hypothalamus controls sleep, thirst, body temperature, hunger, attachment behaviors and more. When your head and brain get banged around in a trauma, these delicate structures can get damaged. My neuroendocrinologist said that they aren't exactly sure why problems occur with the pituitary in head trauma; it may be lack of blood supply to these structures due to trauma, damage to the glands themselves, something else or all of these.

Since my pituitary and hypothalamus are likely damaged, my adrenal glands, which sit just on top of the kidneys, have not been able to produce enough cortisol. I say "likely" because this how it was presented to me. I'm not sure if there really is a way to 100% confirm it or not, other than the blood tests I've already undergone. However, my pituitary doesn't produce enough ACTH, which tells my adrenals to produce cortisol. This is one of the main reasons for my chronic fatigue. Adrenal insufficiency can result in other symptoms, many of which I had been experiencing, including:[19]

- Extreme fatigue
- Low blood pressure (sometimes fainting)
- Decreased appetite and weight loss
- Darkening of the skin
- Salt craving
- Low blood sugar (hypoglycemia)
- Body hair loss or sexual dysfunction in women
- Depression
- Nausea, diarrhea or vomiting
- Abdominal pain
- Muscle or joint pains
- Irritability

The neuroendocrinologist recommended I take low dose supplemental cortisol in the form of hydrocortisone to make up for what my pituitary cannot tell my adrenals to produce. Yep, the hormone most people are trying to get rid of is the one I'm having to take. Kind of funny, I think. Have my symptoms improved since starting medication? Yes, though it took time. I went from utterly exhausted to just feeling tired, which is a huge improvement. I even feel energetic at times. It's such a good feeling to have more energy to do the things I want and need to do in my life. There are still some things that haven't improved yet, but there are many variables. Being a human is complicated, and so is our physiology. When one hormone gets thrown off, it often takes many others with it.

What have I learned from my pituitary? Not only has it taught me more about my hormones and endocrine physiology than I probably ever wanted to know, it's taught me some valuable life lessons.

My pituitary has taught me first and foremost that sometimes life knocks us around, sometimes hard, and we get damaged, yet we continue doing the best we can with whatever circumstances we're in. We keep going, even if it's not how we used to do things under different circumstances. We have a purpose in this life, and we must keep living and pursuing that purpose until it's fulfilled, however that looks to you.

Second, we often need support from the outside. Though we might think we can do everything on our own, like produce a majority of the body's hormones, we need support. We need a team, a network, a tribe, to help us get where we want and need to go in life. When we are down, we can turn to others, just like the supplemental cortisol, to help lift us up and pick up the slack when we need it.

Third, not everything goes to plan. Most of us hope that our bodies will work fairly flawlessly during the majority of our lives. Then WHAM! When life or our body's functions go awry, we have two choices: accept it and do what we can to optimize our health and happiness, or stay stuck in denial. I had a really hard time accepting my TBI. I wanted so desperately to be back to the way I was, and I kept reaching and searching for anything and anyone who might be able to help me. Yes, I have been very proactive, and admittedly, at times have tried to do anything to just make it all just go away. Accepting this new information wasn't easy, either, but I made the choice to do what I could to help myself.

Fourth, take it with a grain of salt. When my neuroendocrinologist confirmed what I knew intuitively to be true about my pituitary, I was glad for the confirmation. When I asked, "What can I do to support it and its healing, particularly through nutrition?" He replied, "It likely won't recover." This, at first, sent me bawling. To hear that such an important structure in my brain might never recover was hard to swallow. I didn't want it to be true, yet I knew it was a possibility. Once I stepped back, examined the situation, and breathed, I was able to process this information more rationally. I thought to myself, "How does he know this damage or dysfunction is permanent? It's just his best guess given his experience and the general knowledge he has of these structures right now. C'mon, you have clients all the time that report that their doctors told them this is the best they'd ever be. Then they defy that prediction and see dramatic improvement when they were told it was impossible! You know the body is resilient, and in 10-20 years we'll likely know a whole lot more and have more treatment options for these kinds of things."

My tears slowed, and I realized that there is a dance between accepting what is, while continuing to seek the answers. As one of my dear friends who counseled me through this emotional roller coaster said, "Try it on." Meaning: what if you accept this prognosis for right now? Just accept it, knowing that things can change, and you can "try on" more information and data later.

I decided to take off the metaphorical garment that was my tendency to reach for anything that would erase my TBI and put on acceptance instead. I planned to just stay the course of treatment with my health care team and see what happened. Down the road, if I choose, I can seek more information and perhaps other treatments. For now, I continue to be present and rejoice in the blessings, gifts, lessons and strength that this TBI has given me. Never did I think I would learn so many valuable lessons from this experience, including from my little pituitary gland.

When most people think of a TBI, they think of headaches, memory and cognitive challenges, but we cannot forget about the cascade of effects that also happens that may not even show up for months to years, including potential hormonal changes due to pituitary or other glandular damage. If you've experienced some of the same symptoms as I've described here in this section, discuss them with your doctor at your next visit. There are ways to balance your hormones and sanity and restore peace to your body and life.

PART II

GETTING HELP, ADAPTING
AND MOVING FORWARD

I admit that moving forward with my life since my injuries has not always been easy. At times it has been very, very hard. The hardest part for me was the lack of energy. My self-image had to shift, and by a lot. Going from a Type-A, go-getter personality to lying on the couch for hours at a time did not sit well with me for a long time. I somehow felt that I was weak and "less than" for being depressed, less active, less energetic and outgoing than I had always known myself to be. After a couple years, though, I realized that despite my sense of physical weakness, my grace, tenacity and ability to go with the flow were growing stronger and stronger. My determination to move forward with my life and my goals, and my desire to help others in the same boat, grew stronger than my limitations, yet I learned to respect these challenges and limitations. These challenges, like depression, PTSD, PCS, hormonal imbalances, adrenal insufficiency, and more are my reality. I had to learn how to both accept them and not let them define me. None of this was accomplished on my own or overnight. Surrounding myself with friends, family, community and a fantastic team of health care professionals was, and still is, essential to my continued healing and growth. To all these people and animals (yes, animals too): my deepest and sincerest gratitude.

You may be wondering, "Where do I even start?" This section is dedicated to helping you answer that exact question, starting with establishing your own personal support team.

Surround Yourself with Support

By whom do you do feel most loved and supported? It may be a spouse/partner, parent, friend, or even a pet. These people (and animals) will be some of your greatest assets in healing and living with a TBI. It can be very difficult for those close to you to understand what you have gone through and your current challenges. They may try to understand, but many of them cannot fully grasp your reality unless they have been through it or something similar themselves.

Surround yourself with friends, family, groups, books, etc. that are *sincerely* and *authentically* positive and uplifting when you need it, and who can be real with you when things suck. These people will listen patiently, help you when you ask for it, cry with you, encourage you, and hold your hand literally and/or metaphorically.

As in any relationship, communication is key. Be fully honest with yourself, first, with your emotions and challenges, and convey these to the best of your ability to those in your inner circle. If they do not know what's going on, they won't be able to offer the support you need. Let them know that you just can't handle going out to Susie's birthday party tonight, for instance, or that you need extra time and reminders to complete a task. It's not that you are antisocial, lazy or don't care; it's just too much stimulation and you move a bit slower than you did prior to your TBI. Those closest to you may accept these changes easily, and others may need as much time to adapt as you do. Give your friends and family links to resources, like those shared in this book (and this book itself) to educate them on brain injuries. The Brain Injury Association of America (www.biausa.org) even has a section on their website for family and caregivers. The more they know, the better they can support and help you. It's possible that not everyone in your circle will make the effort to try to understand or help. This can be very frustrating, and you may even feel hurt when those you thought were your best supporters turn out not to be. As difficult as it may be, let these people go, without judgement or criticism (sometimes easier said than done), and focus your energy instead on moving forward with those who really do love, care and support you.

On the flip side, you sometimes get the friend, family member or acquaintance who wants to offer a little too much advice. They may sincerely want to help, but if you're not ready or willing to receive unsolicited advice, you have every right to kindly let them know. Tell them that you appreciate their desire to help, and that until you say so, you are not ready to hear what they're offering to share. If you have questions or want to discuss it further, you will let them know. Establishing and maintaining these boundaries from the beginning is essential to your healing process and life. Let me give you an example:

I once had an acquaintance, a friend of a friend whom I don't know well (and who doesn't have a TBI), email me to say, "If you are done with your TBI, remember it's not yours," and proceeded to tell me about a treatment modality that I had already been using for years, even before my TBI. I took their email to mean that if I want to be done with my TBI, all I have to do is decide to be done. Let it go. That's it. Like magic, *poof* it's gone. After feeling angry for a few moments at their lack of understanding my situation, I breathed and reflected before emailing them back. I thanked them for caring enough to reach out and share the information with me, and that I had experienced a lot of success with that modality in my course of treatment and healing. I also wrote that I honor my reality and continue to do a lot of work to ensure that I don't identify myself with my TBI. I thanked them again and ended it in a way that did not invite further conversation on the topic (watch Episode 6 of the #tbidiaries on my Head of Hope YouTube channel). I would have rather this person asked, "How can I support you?" or "I have some insights and recommendations you might find helpful. Would you like to hear about them?" instead of giving unsolicited advice that ultimately irritated me.

Tell people in your life if you need them to just listen, *if* you want their advice, or another way they can support you. Telling them what you want or need will help everyone. People who care about you want to make things better for you, but when they can't, they get uncomfortable. It's their own discomfort in not being able to heal you that usually brings about their unsolicited advice, even if it is well intended.

People will often try to empathize, but their efforts might be ineffective or inappropriate. Empathy is connecting to the *feeling* of an experience, not to the experience itself, but people often get this a little confused in practice. I can't tell you how many times people have said, "Oh, I forget stuff all the time, too. Must just be old age." Being in my thirties, old age is certainly not a factor, and prior to my TBI my memory was fantastic, thank you very much. When hearing these kinds of comments from people, they think they're relating, but they don't hear or understand that it's not about the memory challenges. It's about the *frustration* I have felt knowing that I used to have a good memory, I had an injury, and now I forget things. I am different, and not by choice. At first, I used to get a bit ticked off at these kinds of comments, but then I realized that people are just trying to relate the best they know how, even if it's not exactly helpful or real empathy. Just let it go, and realize they are doing the best they know how, too. These moments can be educational opportunities to share with people what it's truly like to experience what you experience, and how it's different from how they are trying to relate. If you choose to educate, I invite you to do so from a place of love and avoid getting defensive or angry.

Support groups, both online and in-person, can be helpful to your healing process, too. Take caution, however, in support groups. If you decide to join one, ask yourself these questions:

1) Does the group provide you with empowering information and constructive ways to move forward with your life?

2) Or does it seem like a continuous group pity party caught in the victim-mindset cycle?

Support groups are valuable for feeling understood by people who share commonalities and experiencing true empathy. Living with a TBI can feel lonely, because on the outside we appear normal to the rest of the world since our scars aren't usually visible. Being able to share resources, inspiration, a laugh and sometimes a cry with people who "get it" may be just what you need. If you start to feel like the group isn't helping you move forward or providing you the support you need, then it's time to disengage.

Support comes in many forms: from a simple phone call or text message, to snuggling on the couch or in the barn with your favorite animal. Being an animal lover, animals have been a huge part of my healing process. On the many sleepless nights I experienced in the first three years post TBI, my dog and cat were always there, at any and all hours. They would come out to the living room and up on the couch with me when I couldn't sleep. The three of us would cozy up, and their presence was more comfort than words can describe. On the mornings when my depression was at its worst, I would go from my bed to the couch, and sit there in silence with my cat purring on my lap. When I had breakdowns at 3:00 a.m. or 3:00 p.m. with no one else around, my dog and cat were there for me to hug, not caring that my tears dampened their fur.

Even though my love of horses helped get me into this mess, this love also has helped me heal. With the help of equine facilitated coaching, I developed a very strong and special bond with a very special horse who unfortunately passed away in 2016 at the age of 30. He understood me when no human did. No words were needed for our communication, and communicate we did. It may sound crazy but trust me on this. Spending time out at the barn with him was the reprieve I frequently needed from the outside world: for connection, understanding, peace and calm. If you're not an animal person, that's okay. Whether it's a living creature or a stuffed teddy bear, find something to hug when you need it. Give it a try. I bet it will make a difference during the hard times.

Keep a Journal

Keeping a journal was a life saver many times, particularly early on in recovery. Daily journal entries helped me track symptoms, challenges and my emotional state. I brought my journals to doctor appointments, knowing that they'd ask me questions, and sometimes very specific ones, that I couldn't answer without them. Since I could not even remember why I walked into a room in my house at times, trying to remember specifics in the heat of the moment at a doctor's office was out of the question. If remembering things is difficult, and you find yourself asking, "Did I already take that pill this morning? Or was that yesterday?" then writing down when you did such things can help you keep track.

When you start a treatment of any kind, a journal can help you track your progress. Sometimes it's difficult to notice small gains over time when we are so caught up in the moment, focusing on what sucks right now. Looking back at journal entries gives you information on how you were doing six weeks or six months ago compared to how you're doing now. For me, it's encouraging to see look back on my entries from time to time and really appreciate and celebrate how far I've come over the years.

If a work-related or auto accident caused your injuries, a journal is essential to any legal case into which you might enter. Legal considerations will be discussed later in this book, but know that if you're even considering legal action around your TBI, you should start a daily journal as soon as possible.

Just as support groups can be helpful or keep you in a state of self-pity, so, too, can a journal. If journaling your symptoms and challenges makes you feel depressed, frustrated, angry or bitter, then stopping that specific journal and shifting your focus to a gratitude journal instead could help. You could even do both: a journal of symptoms and your current reality, and a separate gratitude journal to help uplift you again. Even on the hardest days, there is always something for which to be grateful, I promise. It may just take a little more effort to see.

Assembling Your Healthcare Team and Getting Treatment

One of the clearest observations I've made on my own healing journey and in writing this book is the immense need for guidance and communication between TBI survivors, healthcare professionals and caregivers, when applicable. Because TBI survivors experience such a vast spectrum of severity of injury and consequences, health care providers have a really hard time knowing what to do with us, especially when symptoms last for months or years. As noted in my own story, the general attitude toward concussions (remember, they are classified as mTBIs) is that you'll be fine within about two weeks. But what if you're not? What if you still struggle? What if you're high-functioning *and* still struggling? What then? Who do you see? Who and what can help? These questions may be going through your head, and my hope is to answer some of them here. In this section I'll share some advice, both from the perspective of patient and licensed health professional, on how to assemble your team. Then we'll dive into the plethora of treatment options, some of which you've likely never heard. Access to some of these modalities and treatment methods will be dependent on variables like your geographic location and financial situation. See what sparks your interest the most. That's usually a good place to start or continue with your healing, adapting and living journey. Remember, if there is a will, there is a way.

ASSEMBLING YOUR HEALTHCARE TEAM

What's most important about your healthcare team is that <u>you</u> feel confident and comfortable with its members. Remember that *you* are a part of this team. *You* are the one in charge of what you pursue, what you do or don't do with your body, and what you do or do not put in it. As you meet and work with practitioners, ask questions. If they do not tell you up front, ask why they recommend a certain modality, supplement, pharmaceutical, etc. and how they think it will help you. Ask about the benefits and potential side effects *before* you begin a treatment, supplement or pharmaceutical. Be sure to ask about the side effects of coming off a supplement or pharmaceutical *before* you start taking it. Remember that even holistic approaches can have side effects. Know, too, that not all side effects are negative. In fact, side effects, like pain relief or better concentration, can be positive.

Here are some questions to ask yourself when you begin working with a practitioner:

- Does your practitioner listen to you?
- Do they truly hear what you're saying?
- Do they treat you with respect?
- Do they talk down to you?
- Do they explain their findings and recommendations in a way that *you* understand them?
- Are they willing to answer your questions and address your concerns?
- If you ask questions or express concerns, do they dismiss them or get defensive?
- How do you feel in their presence? Is it positive, or do they make you want to run out the door?
- Are they willing, with your permission and in accordance to healthcare laws, to communicate and work cooperatively with other members of your healthcare team?
- Are they open and receptive to the approaches, beliefs and values you bring to your care, regardless if they personally share these or not?

It's important to feel like the members of your team are on your side 100%. Though asking questions and expressing concerns are essential to establishing and maintaining your team, be mindful to respect each practitioner's knowledge and experience. There is a difference between curiosity and wanting to be informed as a source of empowerment and being interrogating. Practitioners know a lot about their fields, and they are also human. Honestly, as a licensed health professional, I can say that we don't know everything. A good professional will answer, "I don't know" to a question, and either go in search of the answer or point you in the best direction. More than anything, the members of your healthcare team should listen, care, educate and empower, while treating you with respect and compassion.

Now that you have some pointers on what to look for in your practitioners, let's explore some of the many treatment options that could help you in your recovery from and *living* with a TBI. Are there more modalities and treatment options out there than what are included in this book? Absolutely. After many years since my injuries, even I continue to learn about what is out there in the world. All the treatment options and modalities included in this book are ones I've personally pursued and received—all with positive results. My hope in including these here is to educate you on the many options, both allopathic and holistic, that exist and could help you. Some may be familiar to you, others may not. Even though I am a licensed holistic health professional, I believe in the combination of allopathic and holistic care. Both have their gifts and limitations. Working together, they can truly help you achieve and maintain optimal health.

Each treatment option or modality described below includes a Q &A with a practitioner in their field, each with experience of working with TBI survivors. By including their own words, you can get a better understanding how they and their work could help you.

Your Primary Care Physician

Ready to start putting together your healthcare team? Let's begin with your primary care physician, whether you work with a medical doctor (MD), naturopath (ND), osteopath (DO), internist, or other. Generally, it's recommended you follow up with your primary physician after a concussion/TBI. They will ask details of what happened, what you're experiencing now, and do a physical exam. Depending on their training and approach, they may know a little or a lot about TBIs. Ask them what they know about TBIs and about their experience helping other TBI patients. If their answers and experience are satisfactory to you, great! If not, ask if they know someone local who is an expert or specialist in working with TBI patients. If you're lucky, they'll know someone, but also be prepared for if they don't. If the latter, that's where this book comes in especially handy. You may find it helpful to bring along a family member, partner or close friend to your appointment to take down notes or fill in gaps of information if you are really struggling.

Your primary care physician can be a great first member of your team, as they are usually the first to diagnose any of the challenges you present, from neck pain and headaches to depression and PTSD. Though not always the case, primary physicians often have a broad and more general understanding of many conditions, rather than an expertise. Or their expertise is not related to TBIs, so you may find it advantageous to also work with specialists like the ones included in this book.

Neurologist

Neurology is the study of the brain and nervous system. This includes the autonomic nervous system: your fight, flight or freeze, and rest and digest responses to stimuli, spinal cord, peripheral nerves (including cranial nerves), and how nerves affect soft tissue like muscle.

Your 43 pairs of peripheral nerves connect your brain and spinal cord (your central nervous system) to the rest of your body. These nerves control movement, motor coordination and sensation in your body. You have twelve cranial nerves which originate from the brain and innervate the face, throat, eyes, mouth and tongue, ears, upper back and neck, and even down into the torso and digestive tract. When these cranial nerves get damaged, as they can in a TBI, people can experience problems with their main senses of sight, smell, touch, taste and hearing. They can also experience problems with balance and coordination, from damage to either cranial or other peripheral nerves.

Neurologist are specialists in the brain and nerves. A neurologist can help you with things like:

- Dizziness
- Balance

- Confusion

- Coordination

- Memory

- Problems with or loss of senses like smell, vision, taste, etc.

- Muscle weakness

- Headaches

A neurologist will likely perform both a physical exam and a neurological exam at your initial visit. A neurological exam tests muscle strength, reflexes, coordination, etc. Some will track eye movements, balance, memory and other variables to help determine what parts of your brain and nervous system may be damaged or dysfunctional, and work with you to improve and optimize your cognitive and daily function.

To get more information and accurately diagnose you, your neurologist may order a computed tomography (CT) scan or a magnetic resonance image (MRI) of your brain. These images can indicate internal bleeding (subdural hematoma) and other details of your brain. Note that even though you experience mild to severe symptoms, your scans may reveal a healthy, undamaged brain. Just because your imaging may not reveal anything abnormal does not mean that your symptoms should be dismissed. My personal philosophy on imaging of any kind is this: It's just as important to rule things out as in. If your imaging comes back normal, great! This is a good thing. And if the scan reveals useful information, that is great, too. Regardless of the outcome of any imaging you do, your neurologist can help you with the functional challenges you experience.

I interviewed Dr. David Burns, ND, DC, DACNB, FACFN, who has been applying a functional neurology perspective in his practice since 2003 and has focused on helping TBI patients since 2012. Dr. Burns works with TBI patients who incurred their TBI from sports-related and other trauma, such as car accidents, and focuses on prevention through performance.

Q: How do neurologists help people with brain injuries?

A: *Generally speaking, neurologists help identify the cause of perceived deficits, be they from a functional perspective or disease model. The deficits themselves may be due to outright pathology or may be related to an impairment of function without overt indications of disease.*

A typical medical management approach for TBI would include a documentation of symptoms and the monitoring of reported symptoms with encouragement to rest. The idea of rest being that you are placing a lesser demand on injured systems. Eventually the hope or expectation is that the symptoms will resolve. The presence of no symptoms at rest and with progressive cognitive and physical challenge is considered to indicate that the individual has recovered from the TBI.

Q: How does functional neurology differ from regular neurology?

A: *There have been two general perspectives in neurology when it comes to TBI. Some of the difference is a consequence of the population that ends up in front of the neurologist. With a head trauma, particularly when it is significant, there is of course initial concern for issues that are far beyond a concussion. Acute care of TBI that involves concerns of issues beyond a concussion (e.g. a hemorrhage or fracture) is best handled under the guise of a well-trained emergency medical team with appropriate imaging. This is not always necessary, but when it is, medical neurological assessment is most appropriate. It is their function to ensure that the individual is stable and not in immediate danger. As stated in the previous answer, the general approach medically, once it is determined that there is no injury beyond a concussion, will be for rest and avoidance of various activities (e.g. reading, texting, TV). Medical management, generally speaking, will be a wait and see approach.*

A functional neurology approach to concussion management will likely be a bit more proactive and will consider how aspects, regions, networks, systems of the brain are not working as well as they ought to be. After an appropriate rest period, which would be different depending on circumstances, the patient would be evaluated from a functional perspective. Typically, it is known at this point that the individual doesn't have an ablative lesion (i.e. their CT or MRI is unremarkable) but they are complaining of symptoms or issues that have not resolved with rest. The assessment can take many forms and involve various diagnostics. The degree of deficit considered clinically significant is likely less than would be when considering an ablative lesion or disease. Additionally, patterns of dysfunction are considered. That is, regions do not function independently and so everything is evaluated with the consideration of all the other regions that are connected. Once regions of deficits are identified with outcome measures, interventions are applied, and the aberrant outcome measure is monitored for gains. If no gains are made, then the intervention is modified. It should be noted that the symptoms may in fact resolve but there still may be functional impairment.

Functional neurology focuses on how things are working in the brain, whether that's from disease, injury or other dysfunction. Functional neurology looks at the strengths and weaknesses of areas of the brain, systems and integration of those systems, as well as what influences their integrity, like diet, emotional stress, etc.

Q: What would you want TBI survivors to know about working with a (functional) neurologist?

A: *I would want them to know it's not magic. It requires work and a variable amount of time depending on the individual's circumstances. There should be measurable outcomes that can be tracked and noted to show that gain is happening. Work with a (functional) neurologist should include measurable data, a hypothesis of region of deficit, an intervention and measurable change. If no change, then modifications should be made so that there is change.*

Functional neurology looks at relationships of function. One side of your brain or region might function better than the other, yet both can be "within normal limits." Understand relative deficits as you would relative deficits of strength in a muscle. Strengthen your brain just as you would any other injury to any other body organ or system.

Take heart, sometimes people are lucky to be injured because they could have existing functional deficits without any symptoms. Then they get a TBI and go in for treatment for one thing and find out another. By discovering some of the other challenges and making changes, patients are still better off. Some of my patients have said they feel better after treatment than before their TBI because they've learned concepts and applied them for continued growth and healing.

Your healing and success will depend on a lot of variables, including environment, diet, lifestyle and others, and it's your responsibility to engage in the process. You can sit, degenerate or go forward. Grow in some fashion in spite of (ISO) your TBI. ISO is my new motto.

Neuropsychology

Different from neurology is neuropsychology.[20] Neuropsychology focuses on the relationships between brain function, behaviors, thoughts, and emotions. Since traumatic brain injuries affect all these things, working with a neuropsychologist and undergoing a neuropsychological evaluation could give you data on what is working well in your brain and what needs help, as well as skills to optimize brain function and health.

A neuropsychological evaluation includes a detailed health and educational history intake as well as standardized tests and assessments. These aren't your "fill in the bubble" Scantron® tests from your school days. These tests involve words, numbers, memory, recognizing patterns, attention, problem solving, verbal skills and more. These tests and assessments are designed to provide your neuropsychologist and you with information about what your brain can do in a controlled setting. Your neuropsychologist will administer and proctor the tests, giving you directions and observing you as you take them. Some of these tests may be a piece of cake for you, while others may leave you frustrated. Your responses to each test or assessment are important, but so are your reactions to each task, as this can reveal a lot about your emotional state or ability to control your emotions, something with which some TBI survivors struggle.

Because your results are compared to an average, you'll be able to learn in what cognitive tasks you excel, and which you do not, and compare them to what is considered normal. Using this information, your neuropsychologist will provide you with recommendations to improve and optimize both brain function and your daily life. Neuropsychologists also function as therapists, working with you to adjust to living with a TBI, learn new skills and behaviors, or cope with the emotional challenges we experience.

The challenge I personally see with the evaluation is that you are compared to an average (technically, a standard deviation), and not your personal normal prior to your TBI. Most people wouldn't think of or pay for one of these evaluations when they are young and in the peak of health, prior to anything like trauma or injury happening, so unfortunately, we can't fully compare ourselves in this way to our pre-TBI selves. Also, these tests are performed in a controlled environment, meaning, without outside, real world situations around you. How you respond to these tests in a quiet room may be different than when you're under stress and a deadline at work, having a bad day and running on suboptimal sleep or nutrition. The evaluation does, however, give you a lot of potentially useful information to indicate the parts of your brain that may be challenged as a result of your injuries, what to do about it, and both the cognitive and emotional support you may desire.

I had the following interview with my neuropsychologist:

Q: How does neuropsychology help people with brain injuries?

A: *Brain injuries, such as mild traumatic brain injuries (mTBI)/concussions, are often accompanied by cognitive changes. The majority of people post-concussion do not experience any lasting cognitive impairment, though some people will have a more chronic recovery period. Neuropsychological testing can be very helpful in this case, as often times other ways of measuring injury (like a brain scan) will be normal. Cognitive testing can give information about a person's* functional *deficits across lots of different cognitive domains (e.g., memory, attention, processing speed, executive functioning, language).*

Using standardized, objective tests, we can identify areas of deficits otherwise difficult to measure outside of self-report. This is helpful for treatment planning (e.g., within cognitive remediation therapy with a speech therapist). For example, my patients may come in complaining of memory disturbance, and testing shows strong intact memory but poor attention which is secondarily impacting memory through poor attention/learning. In this case, focusing on strategies for improving attention and considering medications for attention would be reasonable treatment options. Cognitive testing is also important to track progress over time by getting a baseline of cognitive abilities, and then re-testing over a recovery period. Neuropsychology also focuses on emotional functioning; changes in mood are common post-TBI, and these often need to be treated as well with either talk therapy or medication options. Mood can, and also does, impact cognitive functioning. Psychoeducation around injury is also important. There is a lot of misinformation out there about concussion/TBI, and it is important to make sure patients have up-to-date information and a clear treatment plan.

Q: How would you describe neuropsychology to someone who has never heard of or experienced it?

A: *Neuropsychology is a specialty field of psychology focused on standardized cognitive and mood assessment of functioning associated with neurologic conditions. It is focused on brain-behavior, with a stress on behavior. These conditions can be neurodevelopmental (like with ADHD or a learning disability) or related to injury or neurodegenerative conditions. It takes a holistic approach in that it considers neurocognitive functioning (thinking) and psychological factors (mood, etc.) in terms of brain-based illness/injuries. Most clinical neuropsychologists will focus on cognitive assessment primarily, though often will see patients for talk therapy also. Typically, this is in the context of neurologic conditions, though not exclusively.*

Q: What would you want TBI survivors to know about neuropsychology and working with a neuropsychologist?

A: *Often a referral to a neuropsychologist comes a little later in recovery—six months post or so. This is a reasonable time frame for the brain to show spontaneous healing. The reason that comprehensive testing is not typically carried out earlier (though often some brief testing is done) is because we know that over time your brain will heal without much intervention at all, and we don't want to put you through a lot of testing that in a few months will not accurately reflect your functioning. So it is okay that this is later.*

I also spend a lot of my time with my patients on education—there are a lot of factors that can impact cognitive functioning, including sleep disturbance, mood factors, pain, chronic fatigue and medications. Unfortunately, many of these symptoms can come with a head injury, depending on how the injury occurred (i.e., if you fall and also injure your back). It is important for patients to understand these factors. Attributing all cognitive changes post-injury to brain injury is likely inaccurate and often limits recovery—these factors also need to be addressed in a treatment model. I would also like my patients to know that mood changes do not mean their symptoms are "all in their head." Mood is regulated by the brain...by this logic everything is "in the head." Psychological functioning is a very important piece in recovery.

Counseling and Coaching

Adapting to life with a TBI isn't always easy, and getting professional support can literally be a life saver. Not only are depression, post-concussion syndrome (PCS), emotional dysregulation and personality changes some of the possible challenges TBI survivors face, but so are the challenges of career/ work, family and social life.

Your emotional health is just as important as your brain function and overall physical health. They are all intimately intertwined more than most of us realize. As I mentioned in in my own story, recovering from and living with a TBI can feel lonely at times, because we often appear normal on the outside to the rest of the world, when we're really struggling on the inside. A qualified and compassionate counselor or coach can help you with the emotional coping and adapting required to keep moving forward with your life.

Depression is the most common mental health challenge associated with a TBI, and it often shows up within the first year.[21,22] When the brain gets damaged, there are changes to one's neurochemistry, including neurotransmitters like serotonin, which is often associated with mood regulation. Antidepressants, supplements, along with exercise, diet and lifestyle, in addition to counseling or coaching, may also help reduce depressive symptoms (we'll go more into nutrition later).

You may have mixed feelings about counseling. It depends a lot on how you've been conditioned to think about mental health and your own personal experiences with counselors or coaches in the past. Know that depression, anxiety, PTSD or other challenges are nothing to be ashamed of. They are very common among not only TBI survivors, but so many people in our society in general. When deciding to work with a mental health professional, whether a licensed mental health counselor (LMHC) or a certified coach, such as a life coach, choose someone with whom you feel truly good talking. Just as with your other providers, ask them about their experience working with TBI survivors. If their experience is satisfactory to you and you feel like you have a good rapport, then you've likely found a good match.

A counselor or coach can help you navigate changes in your life that happen as a result of your injuries, like needing to modify or change careers, or stop working all together if needed. Relationships with family and friends can get strained after your TBI because of things like depression, PCS, PTSD and/or personality changes and the lack of understanding by those you know. These kinds of life changes require as much support as possible. These professionals are there to help when times get tough and you need someone to talk to.

Karin Schenkel is a former neuropsychologist/psychotherapist who transitioned into and currently practices Equine Facilitated Counseling/Coaching. She has extensive experience working with patients with TBIs and has witnessed how the combination of thorough knowledge of brain function, trauma and psychology, applied to coaching with the use of horses, improves TBI survivors' lives.

Q: How does counseling or coaching help people with brain injuries?

A: *Patients with traumatic brain injuries often feel as if a part of themselves, a part of who they were before the accident, is gone, sometimes forever. They not only go through a long period of accepting and adjusting to a new reality and to a daily life that might be different than before, they also have to grief their "old self" and accept their new one. As this is most often not a "better version" of the old self, it is a very hard process to go through. It is comparable to the six stages of the grieving process (shock and denial, guilt, anger, depression, working through, acceptance). During this process, strong emotions are difficult to deal with and process without the help and guidance of a professional.*

Q: What is the difference between a counselor and a coach?

A: *The main difference is the background and the licensing. Counselors/Psychologists treat people with mental illnesses. A client who sees a coach has no diagnosed mental illness. The reason for seeing a coach is to work toward a specific goal, let's say, a career change. The coach explores with the client the different reasons for the change, the possibilities, obstacles that hold the clients back etc. There are sub goals to be set and the client is held accountable by the coach. Coaching can be done on the phone, and often is. The coach primarily works by asking questions to move the client forward. Emotions are not in the main focus of a coaching relationship. If the coach notices a mental problem, he/she is required to refer the client to a counselor. Even if the coach has a background in counseling or psychology, it is unethical to mix the two approaches.*

A patient who sees a counselor or psychologist is in emotional distress, goes through a crisis, is diagnosed with a mental illness and the goal is to treat this. The approach depends on the background of the professional. Emotions are mostly in the center of the treatment. However, the focus can also be on behavioral issues, habits, dysfunctional behavior, etc.

Both counseling and coaching don't do the work for the client/patient. By asking the right questions, the professional helps the client/patient to open up new perspectives and see problems, obstacles, and possibilities in a different light.

Q: How would you suggest selecting a counselor or coach?

A: *I highly recommend working with a therapist who has neurological knowledge. Depending on the brain area that is affected by the injury, patients show different symptoms. As their daily life is sometimes highly compromised by the brain injury, it is pivotal to understand what can trigger severe symptoms. I, for example, treat a patient whose occipital lope (visual center) has been compromised and whenever she engages in visually demanding tasks, she develops a severe migraine which then sets off an anxiety reaction that can lead to a panic attack. She loves sewing, reading and writing, but if she does all that on the same day, it is way too much input for her brain. Just by going through daily activities and seeing what needs to be balanced helped her tremendously. Just being able to explain to a patient that her symptoms are physical and that she is not "a crazy person" takes pressure off. With knowledge in neuropsychology and brain function, part of the treatment can be geared toward brain recovery by implementing specific exercises.*

Besides that, the most important thing is the relationship between the patient and the therapist. Therefore, I recommend to always ask for a trial session. Also, the therapist should have experience with brain injuries.

Q: Many people are ashamed or wary of seeing a LMHC or working with a coach. What would you say to someone who feels this way?

A: *If you break your leg, you seek help in order for your leg to be treated by a professional so that it can heal. The same applies to brain injuries. As the brain is not only a "physical organ," like a leg or an arm, that can be treated by a physician, but regulates emotions, controls our behavior, pretty much defines who we are, or let's say, regulates our mental health status, a mental health specialist must be part of the treatment team. Patients are sometimes still concerned that they are stigmatized because they are in treatment. However, each and every person who seeks help, talks about it, and benefits from mental health interventions should speak out so that nobody has to be ashamed anymore.*

Q: What would you want TBI survivors to know about getting counseling or coaching and working with an LMHC or coach?

A: *Recovering from a TBI can sometimes be a very long process. The brain recovers, but it might take years. Depending on the areas that have been compromised and the severity of the injury, there might never be a full recovery. My advice is to live in the moment and enjoy every little step forward. Don't get discouraged, if it seems like a step forward and two back again. Adjust to your new reality and your new life and accept it, which doesn't mean that you have to settle and stop fighting.*

Neurolink®

Among some of the treatment options mentioned in this book of which you may not have ever heard is Neurological Integration System (NIS), or Neurolink®.[23] Admittedly, explaining Neurolink®, like many other modalities I share here in this book, can be a challenge, but trust me, it works! Think of booting up your computer. If there is something not communicating or working quite right, your computer may start up very slowly, or incorrectly. When all the wires and circuits are connected and communicating, you and your computer function optimally. NIS works similarly to selecting "restart" on your computer. Neurolink® addresses the many types of stresses that we encounter both daily and resulting from trauma, including physical and emotional stress and even infections. NIS effectively helps to reset proper signaling of neuropathways, clears pathogens from the immune system and can bring harmony back to the brain and nervous systems.

Neurolink® is a hands-on modality using light touch with you, the client, fully clothed, and lying on a massage treatment table. This modality is far from massage in application but is also very relaxing. After a detailed health history intake, a Neurolink® practitioner will test your neurological pathways with a diagnostic technique called muscle testing[24] that simply tests muscle strength when certain pathways are touched. Once your practitioner knows where they need to work, you may be asked to place a hand on a certain part of your body, like the back of your head or on your sternum (chest), while your practitioner briefly touches another place or two at the same time. Then, they'll reassess though muscle testing and see what has changed. Where they touch and what you report as your symptoms may seem unrelated to the untrained layperson, when in fact they are indeed related.

Daniel Lane, Certified NIS practitioner since 2007, shared this about Neurolink® and working with people with TBIs:

Q: How does Neurolink® help people with brain injuries?

A: *Trauma causes inflammation, both acute and sometimes long-term, low grade, chronic inflammation. Inflammation causes signal disruption in the body and brain. It is this signal disruption between the brain and the injured cells that allows the inflammation to persist. Multiple studies have shown that inflamed cells, including injured brain cells from concussion and other injuries, do not metabolize properly. Their functions are disrupted. This explains why in a recent trial of curcumin, an extract of the spice turmeric, outperformed both Prozac and placebo in the treatment of moderate to severe depression. Once the inflammation is brought under control, normal function can resume. NIS seeks to find and correct this signal disruption.*

Q: How would you describe a session to someone who has never heard of or experienced Neurolink®?

A: *Basically, if the brain is not fully aware of an issue, it's not going to address it properly. The brain gets millions of messages every second. If there is a disruption of these messages between the brain and an organ or tissue, there will be a less than optimal response. There can be various reasons the brain does not get these messages: infection, trauma, chemical exposure, emotional stress, etc. When you visit an NIS practitioner we go through the body like a 60,000-mile check on the car. Through use of a muscle testing procedure (a signal feedback loop) we check digestion, the immune system, ligaments, tendons, hormones, emotional stress* *defaults, etc. Once a signal disruption is detected, we stimulate a specific part of the brain called the postcentral gyrus to re-establish communication between the brain and the affected area. It is gentle and non-invasive.*

Q: What would you want TBI survivors to know about Neurolink® and working with an NIS practitioner?

A: *I would want anyone dealing with TBI or similar situation to know that NIS has helped many people with those issues. Many times, people have improved when other approaches and modalities have failed to produce significant results. And the down side is...nothing. You cannot harm anyone with NIS. The worst that can happen is a person does not respond.*

EMDR

If your TBI resulted from a traumatic event, like a car accident, fall, or violence, EMDR could be extremely helpful. Even if your TBI was not caused by a traumatic event in the opinion of others or society, if it was traumatic to *you* and/or you have been diagnosed with post-traumatic stress disorder (PTSD), you will likely benefit from Eye Movement Desensitization and Reprocessing (EMDR). EMDR helps people who have experienced trauma to release oneself from the emotional story of a specific traumatic event and see it more objectively, like seeing the trees through the forest, as opposed to staying lost in that forest.

EMDR is a form of psychotherapy, though it involves significantly less talking than traditional therapy. The practitioner doesn't interpret your experience and emotions for you, but rather supports you in your own processes of healing through this specific protocol. EMDR helps you reframe psychological trauma and the emotions around an event from anger, fear, hopelessness, etc., to empowerment, confidence and strength.

Though psychotherapy/counseling and coaching are essential in recovery and adapting to life with a TBI, what I loved about my EMDR sessions was that I didn't have to talk as much about how I felt. Since I was struggling with PTSD after the car accidents in particular, though the fall from the horse was traumatic, too, EMDR helped me get out of my constant fight or flight mode. Personally, I did not use eye movements all the time. Instead, I used pulsers that alternately vibrated between my right and left hands to get the bilateral (both sides) stimulation of my brain as we went through the process. This worked better for me than the eye movements and it was nice to have options.

The eight-phase EMDR[25] process may not make a lot of sense to the lay person, but sometimes you don't need to fully understand to know *how* something works, only that it *does*. EMDR practitioners are typically experienced licensed mental health counselors (LMHCs), PhDs, or other qualified degrees and distinctions. As with any practitioner with whom you consider working, ask first about their experience working with TBI survivors so that you find a practitioner you trust.

Barbara Goff, Licensed Professional Counselor (LPC), trained in EMDR 2008 and certified in 2010, has specialized in helping clients heal from trauma since 1986. Integrating EMDR, art therapy, relaxation, breath work as well as essential oils in her practice, Barbara answered these questions about EMDR:

Q: How does EMDR therapy help people with brain injuries?

A: *EMDR is a comprehensive treatment approach created in 1989 by Dr. Francine Shapiro (PhD) to deal with PTSD specifically. Since this time, EMDR has gone through rigorous evidence-based research in many domains to test the effectiveness of the approach. It has been given the stamp of approval by the American Psychological Association, the American Psychiatric Association, Veterans Association, and the NIH. Though it is now considered a full treatment approach such as Cognitive Behavioral, Gestalt, Family Systems Therapy and so forth, it is one of the most vigorously tested protocols. While there are understandings about its effectiveness, science is still working to find out what is truly happening in the brain and human experience. Many people with brain injuries also suffer with PTSD from their injuries. Addressing the unresolved trauma* can help restore peace and significantly reduce PTSD symptoms.

EMDR is an eight-phase model that incorporates the past, present and future concerns of individuals. The use of the Bilateral Stimulation in the treatment is thought to bring about the effect of lowering arousal and desensitizing traumatic memories, images, flashbacks and sensations. The therapeutic relationship is considered very important in the work and in building sufficient resources within an individual to be able to tolerate strong responses. In working with people with brain injury and seizures, having coordination of care and thorough assessment including consultation with medical and helping professionals in other treatment modalities is critical. EMDR Therapy can evoke very strong emotions as an experience is reprocessed. The clinician will help the client by strengthening his or her inner resources to manage strong emotions and assure choice and control during the reprocessing.

Q: How would you describe EMDR to someone who has never heard of or experienced it?

A: *EMDR is a powerful experience of change happening in the brain and body during and continuing after EMDR sessions. I found EMDR to be surprising, unexpected, and amazing, as the brain seemed to go where it needed to go and make images, and sensations on its own as the processing was happening. In my own experience going through EMDR, I often shook my head and said, "How is this happening? What's happening?" but I knew for a fact that change for the better was occurring. Slowly and sometimes rapidly, the often very strong sensations, images, thoughts and experiences seemed to alter and shift without my own effort or thought, in the unconscious. At times it was emotionally powerful, and other times laughable and funny. But the brain changed, and experience changed. The brain knew what it needed to do and with EMDR, the brain and body were freed up to do just what needed to be done to heal.*

Q: What would you want TBI survivors to know about EMDR and working with an EMDR therapist?

A: *Most of all, EMDR therapy is a collaboration between the client and therapist and the work is always in the full control of the client and to serve what is best for the client. Clients are instructed with the ability to give a "stop" signal at any time, and the work proceeds with full awareness by the client and therapist that the client is directing the work.*

CranioSacral Therapy

Did you know that the bones in your head move? It's true. The cranium (skull) must essentially "breathe" to accommodate the ebb and flow of cerebral spinal fluid (CSF) as it travels up and down the spinal cord and around the brain in an ideally rhythmic way. This CSF rhythm can be felt in the head, the sacrum at the bottom of the spine, and in other areas of the body. When the cranial bones or sacrum get out of their optimal alignment, it affects the flow of the CSF and the overall function of your body. Hitting your head or having a bad fall on your bum not only disrupts this flow but can also create compression in the head (have you ever felt like your head is in a vice?), negatively impacting brain and bodily function.

Thankfully, there is a modality called CranioSacral therapy (CST) that can help realign the cranial bones and restore a healthy CSF rhythm. Through subtle, very gentle touch, CST helps to normalize the fluid and membrane system around the brain and spinal cord, allowing the body to heal and function optimally. CranioSacral therapy is very relaxing to receive and is very effective in addressing a lot of the symptoms TBI survivors experience, like headaches, neck and other body pain, brain fog, loss of senses like taste, smell and more. [26]

Kathleen Yow-Wells, LMT and Certified Biodynamic CranioSacral Therapist since 1998 answered the following questions about CranioSacral Therapy and TBIs:

Q: How does CranioSacral therapy help people with brain injuries?

A: *CranioSacral therapy reduces inflammation in the brain allowing the membranous sutures between the skull bones to relax restrictions and/or compressions caused by the concussion. This assists the brain to settle back into the buoyancy of the fluids in the skull. It assists to release the shock and trauma the system is holding onto from the physics of impact. This allows the sympathetic and parasympathetic nervous system to relax and rebalance. CST helps alleviate pain, headaches, vision disturbances, and that 'pressure' feeling in the head. Following concussion, CST gently and gradually restores disrupted sleep patterns, cognitive functioning, neck/shoulder tension, and other lingering symptoms. Often a high degree of frustration is present as daily activities, careers, and lifestyle are all greatly affected. CranioSacral helps the patient to experience Dynamic Stillness or as I like to say, "Deep, profound, significant relaxation where health is restored." It helps reduce the physical and emotional symptoms, including anxiety and depression.*

Q: How would you describe CranioSacral therapy to someone who has never heard of or experienced it?

A: *CranioSacral therapy is from the osteopathic tradition. It's non-invasive, gentle, yet extremely powerful AND effective. You lay on a massage table face up, very comfortable, and that's all the patient has to do. CST consists of gentle 'holds' anywhere on the body. With concussion patients, I usually start with a hold on the sacrum and work my way up to the neck, skull, and brain. I'm listening to the pulse that's created by the cerebrospinal fluid circulating up the spine, into the brain, and back down the spine. I monitor this cranio rhythmic impulse (CRI) by listening with my hands and following the movement into the pattern. The system begins to correct itself, however needed, be it fascia, bones, and/or sutures (joints between bones of the skull). You will experience deep relaxation, often to the point where you feel like you've taken a long satisfying nap. You may hear stomach gurgles, feel twitching or jerks as your body begins to release the stored trauma. I find the effects to continue for about 36 hours while the body is integrating the changes.*

Q: What would you want TBI survivors to know about CranioSacral therapy and working with a CranioSacral practitioner?

A: *My experience in working with concussions and CranioSacral therapy demonstrates it is extremely effective for brain injuries, both acute and chronic. There are two schools of CranioSacral therapy: Biomechanical and Biodynamic. What are the differences? For the sake of brevity, biomechanical instigates changes in the body, whereas in biodynamic CranioSacral, we simply make contact with the system through the CranioSacral rhythmic impulse and wait: Wait for the system to relax, repair, and restore. I often say to patients, "Your system created all this compensation; it knows how to release these patterns when given a chance." Both schools are valuable and work well together. I always suggest working with a Certified CranioSacral Therapist when recovering from a TBI.*

Chiropractic Care

Your brain is not the only thing affected in a TBI. Accidents, falls, or other means of blunt force to the head affect the whole body, not just the areas that were hit. Many TBI survivors experience neck and/or back pain and headaches, both immediately after their injuries and sometimes chronically, if left untreated. Working with a doctor of chiropractic (DC), aka chiropractor, can help relieve musculoskeletal pain and headaches and restore lost range of motion to the spine and other joints. Though chiropractic care has become mainstream for many people as part of their healthcare, it is still considered fringe by some and misunderstood by others.

Due to trauma or repetitive habits, the spine and other joints can lose mobility, affecting the nervous system, overall function and range of motion. A chiropractic adjustment includes gentle spinal manipulation that can help restore mobility, range of motion, function and comfort to the body.

Chiropractors offer a hands-on approach to addressing the health of the spine and the whole person. Chiropractors use an array of diagnostic tools and skills to bring about better function and comfort to their patients, all without the use of pharmaceutical drugs. They are also able to assist in therapeutic exercises, nutrition and lifestyle advice. [27]

Like many modalities, there are many styles of chiropractic care. Some approaches are extremely gentle, while some are more assertive. Some chiropractors only adjust the upper cervical vertebrae (neck spine), while others work with the whole body. Most adjustments feel good and are very effective in relieving pain, restoring range of motion and function and enhance overall well-being.

I interviewed Dr. Carrie Babcox, DC, who has been in practice since 1999, about chiropractic care as a treatment option for TBIs:

Q: How would you describe chiropractic care and how it can help people with brain injuries?

A: *Chiropractic care is the restoration of body balance from joint, muscle, soft tissue and/or nervous system dysfunction. The body can become imbalanced from physical, chemical and mento-emotional stresses. Through chiropractic work, balance of these three systems can be returned. Chiropractic care is an effective way of not just dealing with symptoms of TBI but restoring the system to a growth and repair state, which is healing. Since TBI can vary from mild to severe, it is best to initiate chiropractic care once our medical counterparts deem the patient to be stable. Think of medical doctors as the firefighters putting out fires and chiropractors as the carpenters, looking to restore and rebuild a system to health again. While technically the two could exclusively co-exist, in order to completely regain health, they both must fulfill their role. MDs have heroic life-saving measures. Chiropractors have a long-term focus of repair and regeneration. In the case of TBI, there is no quick fix, but persistence over time is where lasting benefit is achieved.*

TBI is an impact of the brain inside the skull, the sliding of the brain tissue against the skull bones and tissue lining these bones. There are three main areas of the body that a chiropractor will focus on in the case of TBI: the atlas (first cervical or neck vertebrae in the spine), the cranial bones (skull) and the sacrum or tailbone. A chiropractor is an expert in both assessing dysfunctional motion in these areas as well as restoration of function to these very same structures.

"So why is it important for bones and soft tissues to be moving properly to

heal up my brain?" you might ask. The answer is, if the bones of the skull, atlas and sacrum are locked, they decrease the fuel delivery, blood supply and nerve supply to the brain.

In a healthy brain and nervous system, there is a loop of communication between the brain and the tissues of the body. The skull is the bone surrounding and protecting the brain, the spine is the bone that surrounds and protects the spinal cord and nerves. The spine and spinal cord create the superhighway of information between the body and brain. So, it makes sense to have a protective case of bone around these vital structures! As a result of the trauma that occurs during a brain injury, these bones can become locked and rigid, altering the information going up to the brain which then affects the information coming out of the brain.

The brain and spinal cord are encased and protected by a nutrient-rich fluid called cerebrospinal fluid, or CSF. The pump for CSF is created through coordinated cranial and sacral movements. If one or both of these areas are restricted in motion, then the pumping action cannot occur and CSF becomes stagnant. CSF is vital to bring nutrition to the brain, and also take away toxins that will keep the brain from healing. Another pump in the body, which keeps blood flowing, is the heart. With CSF flow, there is not a heart to pump the fluid, but rather the pump is through subtle motions of the bones of the skull and the tailbone. Again, the flow of CSF is VITAL to proper brain function. The atlas bone of the spine, on which the skull sits on top, can also become restricted to the point that it impedes proper cerebrospinal fluid flow. These bone and joint restrictions inhibit proper flushing and ridding of a buildup of fluid in the brain.

Q: How would you describe a session to someone who has never experienced chiropractic care?

A: *Most chiropractors begin with an initial exam, which includes a health history intake and a thorough physical examination, including range of motion assessments. Some chiropractors use x-rays and other electronic assessment tools, too, as part of the initial exam.*

Once the initial exam is done, the session will focus on restoring motion to restricted joints and soft tissues. With TBI, treatments are very gentle, safe and effective. Care will be taken by the doctor of chiropractic to meet your body where it is for the day and not exceed what you need for that day. You will likely feel gentle pressure on joints and soft tissues. This is to effectively adjust or manipulate the bony position and soft tissues to restore motion. The use of hands or tools to perform this will vary per doctor. Always expect to be comfortable. If not, let the doctor know what you are feeling. Therefore, it is important to find a chiropractor who is willing to listen to you and the story your body's joints and tissues are telling the doctor.

Structural Integration

Structural Integration (SI)[28] is a hands-on, therapeutic modality especially effective in treating chronic pain and restoring optimal alignment and function in the body. Structural Integration focuses on fascia, the connective tissue matrix in the body. Fascia is the web like tissue that surrounds and permeates muscles, nerves, organs, blood vessels and bones. When you experience physical or emotional trauma and its resulting compensation, as well as repetitive movements or lack of movement, this can cause fascia to lose its elasticity. When this tissue becomes "stuck," it creates imbalances in our skeletal alignment, causing pain and dysfunction. SI addresses your fascia to restore alignment, function, ease and comfort back to your body.

Structural Integration may at first sound similar to massage or physical therapy. In some ways it is because the practitioner uses their hands and your movement to help you change your body. The difference with SI is that it is done in a series of strategic sessions, usually 10-12, depending on which school your practitioner attended, to address your entire body. The goal of SI is to change dysfunctional alignment and movement patterns in the whole body for lasting relief from chronic challenges, rather than chasing symptoms.

As a Board Certified Structural Integrator (BCSI) since 2011, I share my own professional insights on how SI can help TBI survivors:

Q: How does Structural Integration help people with brain injuries?

A: SI can help TBI survivors with chronic pain and limitations from things like neck and back pain, headaches and jaw pain, to name a few, that are associated with their initial injuries or which have developed afterwards. This can include stiffness, muscle pain, joint pain and nerve pain, from mildly irritating to debilitating.

When trauma occurs, the entire body is affected, not just the place of impact, such as the head in the case of a TBI. Following a TBI, a person's head usually gets the most attention, and rightfully so. If their head isn't properly aligned and supported by the entire body below, then neither the body nor the brain can function optimally. The head itself often gets compressed and misaligned on the neck due to the force of the initial blow or impact. This force is transferred into the entire body through the myofascial (connective tissue) system, leading to collapse in places, compensation patterns in posture and movement, limited range of motion on both a small and large scale, and eventually pain. Structural Integration addresses a person's individual alignment pattern to achieve optimal support, space, range of motion and comfort in his or her body. SI can also help TBI survivors feel more connected and 'at home,' in their bodies. After trauma and the many challenges TBI survivors face, people can feel almost alienated from and at war with their bodies. Structural Integration can give you a better understanding of what is happening in your whole body, teach how to break dysfunctional habits and replace them with better ones (like how you sit at your computer), help you feel wholeness and ease again, with less pain and better movement for months and years ahead.

Regarding going through an entire SI series, I recommend pursuing SI six months to a year after the TBI occurred. Individual bodywork sessions with an SI practitioner are indicated and helpful sooner than this once the client is cleared by their physician to receive treatment. Other modalities are more appropriate in the immediate, acute stages of healing. SI excels with the chronic limitations, aches and pains.

Q: How would you describe a session to someone who has never experienced SI?

A: *After a thorough intake and conversation about health history, current challenges and goals, the practitioner does a visual, and often hands-on, assessment. The client is in minimal clothing: usually modest undergarments or shorts and a bra or tank top (for women). The practitioner will observe the client in a standing position, looking at the client from the front, back and both sides to discern where they need to work that day and in the future. The client will likely spend most of the session on a massage treatment table, with the practitioner doing hands-on work in certain areas and asking the client to move parts of their body at times. The client's movement, such as bending and straightening a knee or simply taking a deep breath, helps engage and change the fascial (connective) tissue under the practitioner's hands. In this way, the client and practitioner work together to make the changes. There is almost always neck and back work (done seated) in every session, regardless of the areas of focus for that day. Most sessions will include awareness and movement education to help clients maintain and progress their changes further.*

Q: What would you want TBI survivors to know about Structural Integration and working with an SI practitioner?

A: *I want TBI survivors to know that Structural Integration can potentially alleviate chronic pain that often accompanies brain injuries, like headaches, neck and back pain. It can potentially improve brain function by working with the cranium itself. Not only is this modality very effective in relieving chronic pain and restoring movement and function, it can help clients feel "connected" in their body again. SI works with and affects nearly every system in the body. Therefore, it is much more than treating symptoms; it's about optimizing function and wholeness so people can live their best life.*

Acupuncture

You've likely heard of acupuncture and that it involves placing needles in the body, but did you know it can help TBI survivors? Acupuncture uses the insertion of thin, sterile needles into specific points of the body to bring about a physiological change. In Traditional Chinese Medicine, there are lines of energy flow in the body called meridians. Acupuncture points, where needles are placed, follow along these meridians, which are correlated to parts of the body like organs, glands, etc. When energy gets blocked in these meridians, it results in pain, dysfunction and illness.[29] Some acupuncturists also use manual techniques like acupressure or cupping, or application of heat to enhance the treatment.

Acupuncture, used for optimizing health for millennia, has been clinically proven to be effective in treating chronic pain, hormone imbalances, PTSD, depression, reducing stress, and so much more. These challenges are extremely common for TBI survivors. Acupuncture is extremely relaxing and painless. It's rare to even feel the extremely thin needles being expertly placed. If you're afraid of needles, know that the needles used in acupuncture are much thinner than the hypodermic needles used to administer vaccinations. Therefore, you rarely feel them.

Tracey Steger, EAMP, LAc, is an East Asian medicine practitioner and licensed acupuncturist trained at the Seattle Institute of East Asian Medicine. She helps her patients find the root causes of their diseases and lead more harmonious and pain-free lives. I asked Tracey some questions about acupuncture:

Q: How does acupuncture help people with brain injuries?

A: *After a traumatic brain injury, acupuncture can be helpful in calming the nervous system, restoring neurological function, and promoting the body to heal itself. Acupuncture has been shown to affect the neurochemical function of the brain (even from inserting a needle into the foot!), and can change brain patterns that result in anxiety, fear, and pain. Acupuncture is also beneficial for symptoms associated with TBI—such as depression, PTSD, sleep disorders, migraines, and headaches.*

Q: How would you describe acupuncture to someone who has never heard of or experienced it?

A: *Acupuncture is one method of treatment under the umbrella of East Asian medicine. Your practitioner will first interview you about your symptoms and also your health, in general. Although the practitioner is treating your brain injury, it's important to understand the patient as a whole—physically, mentally, and emotionally. After feeling your pulse, looking at your tongue, and possibly palpating different acupuncture points on your arms and legs, your practitioner will begin inserting thin filiform needles into specific acupuncture points. Most patients are surprised by how painless it is, and many find it relaxing and will even fall asleep during treatment.*

Q: What would you want TBI survivors to know about acupuncture and working with an acupuncturist?

A: *Be sure to find a licensed acupuncturist/East Asian medicine practitioner. Don't hesitate to call a potential acupuncturist to see if it would be a good fit, or you can ask for a consultation. Expect that the acupuncturist will want to treat you 1-2 times per week, for at least 6-8 weeks and possibly more. Most insurance plans cover acupuncture.*

Where Do You Start?

There are certainly other modalities and treatments that I haven't covered here because I haven't yet personally experienced them. I wanted to speak to what I personally know has helped me and has the potential to help you, too. Additional modalities and treatments for you to consider include:

- Neurofeedback
- Biofeedback
- Hyperbaric chamber

- Speech therapy

- Sound healing

- Art therapy

If you're overwhelmed by the list of options included in this book, identify which treatment or modality sparks your interest the most. Pick that one, just one, and start there. You may be tempted to try several at once, or even the entire list, but I urge you, both as a TBI survivor and a licensed health professional, to do only one or two things at a time. That way you can be more objective in knowing if something is helping you or not.

Most of us want instant gratification and relief of our symptoms, and rightfully so. Know that *time* is a huge component of long-term healing and wellness. Give any and all treatments you pursue *time*. One session might do wonders, as they often can, but many of these are processes done over weeks or months, and sometimes, years. Be patient. Be an active participant and partner in your healing. If something doesn't serve you or give you the results you're seeking after some time, assuming you have realistic expectations, know that it may not be what you need at that moment. This doesn't mean that modality or treatment didn't work. Rather, either the practitioner wasn't the best fit for you or something else might serve you better right now.

Treatment for and recovery from a TBI is an investment in time, energy and money, all of which should be used as wisely as possible per your individual situation. If you're in the United States, health insurance companies do cover most of the modalities included in this book. Coverage is determined by your own individual insurance plan, and I encourage you to call your insurance company to find out if they will cover a specific modality *before* you begin treatment. This way you decrease the risk of any surprises about whether a treatment is covered or not. You may need to get some detailed information before you call your insurance company, such as the diagnosis (code) or reason for treatment. In the insurance world, this is called the ICD-10 code. When consulting over the phone with a potential provider, once you've spoken with them about your challenges and goals to see if they're a good fit, ask if they bill and accept your insurance. You might ask them for the CPT code they use to bill. This is the code providers use to indicate the type(s) of treatment used in a session and the duration of the treatment. Having the ICD-10 and CPT codes when you speak to the insurance company might be helpful when verifying your benefits. Many providers do not accept or bill health insurance, so try to see the overall value of a treatment or modality, rather than just the dollar value of your investment. If you get the care you need and experience positive results from a provider or treatment, whether insurance pays for it or not, then I encourage you to invest your time, energy and money into the treatment(s). Remember, **you are worth it**.

Depending on your geographic location, willingness and ability to travel, and other individual circumstances, you may or may not have access to all the modalities included here. Again, start with what resonates with you the most and go from there based on accessibility to providers in these fields.

Help is out there. You are not alone. What will your first, or next, step be? Write it in the space below.

The modality or treatment I want to pursue first is

_____.

Hiring an Attorney

In the instance that your TBI was caused by someone else's negligence, such as an auto- or work-related accident, seeking legal counsel is as essential as your medical treatment. Just like choosing a practitioner with whom to work, finding the right attorney for you might require some shopping around. If your situation requires the help of an attorney to recoup money for incurred medical bills, lost wages, and pain and suffering, then find a reputable attorney experienced in their field, ideally who has represented people with brain injuries in the past and won their cases. In my experience, working with insurance companies, even your own, can be difficult. Consulting an attorney to assist is the best strategy to navigate the industry, especially given the complexity of symptoms resulting from an accident. Dealing with the insurance companies is the last thing you likely want or ought to be doing immediately following a brain injury. Don't trust either insurance company, neither your own nor the one of the other party.

Legal cases can be tricky and complicated. Details matter. This is where keeping your journal can be very useful. Do talk first with your attorney about keeping a journal, because it could be subpoenaed or used in court if requested. Keep your journal and conversations with your providers clear and to the point as much as possible, so that nothing gets misinterpreted or potentially used against you in your case. It's important to describe your symptoms in detail to your providers, such as how they are impacting your professional and personal life. Sometimes patients do not share openly with their providers or, especially for us TBI folks with memory challenges, we forget details. Sometimes providers do not ask for details, either. Sharing openly with your medical providers improves your care and could potentially benefit your case and earn you maximum compensation.

If possible, ask to see your medical records the moment you open a legal case, and again as your treatment and case progress over time. Make sure that what your providers are writing down in your medical file is correct. Chart notes are often correct, but it's good to double check on occasion. It's important to point out that *how* providers word things like your symptoms and their findings in their chart notes can, potentially, make or break your case. Remember, your medical records are *yours* and you can request to see them. Save all medical receipts and statements from your insurance company of claims processed. These statements are called Explanation of Benefits, or EOBs. Track all mileage driven to and from TBI-related medical appointments. Some attorneys will keep track of mileage for you, though it doesn't hurt to record mileage yourself, too. Keep track of any lost time and wages from employment. Keep track of things you miss out on socially because of your injuries, like birthday parties, vacations, weddings, and other events. These are part of your quality of life which is also often factored into settlements.

Avoid posting photos or details of your accident or anything related to your legal case online or on social media, as your accounts can be subpoenaed by a judge. This includes Facebook, Facebook messages, Facebook groups,

Instagram, blogs, etc. Though this can create a lot of stress and anxiety about what to say or what not to say, follow the advice of your legal counsel when it comes to sharing your experiences in any way that is or could be made public. Remember, if the defense can find it or it is subpoenaed, it could be used against you.

Just as with your medical providers, be 100% honest with your attorney. They are there to help you, too, and need full disclosure of your experience to effectively represent you. This is where being your own advocate may not only help your healing, but also help your case. Get educated. Explore the references in the back of this book. Find research articles. Read books and blogs. Ask your attorney if it is okay to send them relevant findings that support your case.

Do not give up or give in quickly. The defense would love this legal experience to be so stressful for you that you settle for anything, and at the first offer. Your case could potentially take years to resolve, so pack your patience and keep fighting for appropriate compensation for your injuries. If you have a legal case, you'll likely experience even greater healing as soon as your case closes. No matter the stress and the inconvenience, do not give up. **You are worth it.**

Self-Care: Filling Your Cup

As important as the care from your health care providers is, your self-care is as important, if not more so. You may have a treatment once a week for an hour, yet there are still 167 hours in the week for you to take charge of your own body, thoughts and actions. Self-care is exactly that: care for yourself in body, mind and spirit. It looks different for each person. Ultimately, self-care is about giving back to yourself so that you can feel and live your best. When you feel your best, you can be the best partner, parent, friend, employee or employer, practitioner, sibling, or whatever role you play.

There are many ways to refill your proverbial cup and there is no right or wrong way to do self-care, so long as you do it. My own definition of self-care includes what I do for myself, as well as getting treatment. After all, we can't do it all ourselves, but there is a lot we can do to support our own healing and well-being. Here are some forms of self-care that I personally have found helpful in both my TBI recovery and life, in case you need some ideas to get you started.

YOGA

Though I became a certified yoga instructor after my TBI, yoga had already been an important part of my self-care for years. For some yogis, the practice is about the physical workout. For others, it's an opportunity to slow down, stretch and be present in their bodies and breath. Both are great reasons to practice. Just know your goal or intention in practicing yoga so that you find a class that helps you achieve that goal. Yoga styles vary tremendously, so it's important to find one (or several) that satisfies your goals and meets your needs.

Since my TBI, there are certain yoga poses that I don't do because they create too much pressure in my head. It's important to let your instructor know about any health conditions you have prior to practicing to ensure they guide you in a safe and enjoyable practice appropriate for your needs and abilities. The most important guideline to remember when you practice is to *do no harm to yourself*. This means modify where you need to and avoid poses that cause pain or feel unsafe to you. Yoga can be a great way to reconnect with your body, move mindfully, and stay present with your thoughts, feelings, body and breath. I find it much harder to focus at times since my TBI, and yoga is one of the ways that helps me stay present and focused while strengthening and stretching my body.

MEDITATION

If you've seen the animated movie *Up*, you might remember the talking dog named Dug. As he's introducing himself to the old man, Carl, Dug gets distracted mid-sentence, and shouts, "Squirrel!" and then continues talking. That's how my brain feels at times: squirrely and easily distracted. A wonderful complement to yoga, meditation can help your mind focus and slow down. Meditation isn't necessarily easy, especially if your mind and thoughts are all over the place like mine.

Meditation can be done sitting in a chair or against a wall, sitting on a meditation cushion or bolster, or even lying down. In most meditation traditions it's done sitting upright, so that the spine is long and comfortable. Sitting like this isn't comfortable or accessible to everyone, so know that having your body comfortable so that you're not distracted by discomfort is key, regardless of the position you choose.

Meditation, in my own view and understanding, isn't the absence of thought, but rather, not getting attached to any one thought. Here's the imagery I use to avoid getting attached to thoughts during meditation: Imagine a conveyor belt floating high up in the sky. On it are your thoughts. You watch each thought pass by in front of you on the conveyor belt, and then fall off the end into infinity.

During my yoga teacher training, I learned another useful image: a goat tied to a post. Imagine your thoughts like the goat tied to a post in the middle of a field. That goat can wander freely on a long rope until you start to rein it in, slowly, getting closer and closer to the post. The goat may get away and wander back to the end of its rope, but you can always gently bring it back to the center.

When you sit in meditation, thoughts will appear, and your mind will wander, just like the goat. Instead of getting upset that you're thinking about something, because you will think, or that your mind has latched on to your grocery list or tomorrow's meeting, just recognize that it happened and bring it back to the here and now.

Begin by just sitting quietly and paying attention to your breath; the inhales and the exhales. Sit quietly for even two minutes if this is difficult for you, and then gradually add more time over days, weeks and months.

Meditation, like learning any skill, is a practice. If you are having a difficult time or have questions about meditation, seek out a meditation teacher in your area. There are even apps you can get on your phone, like Insight Timer, with guided meditations on select topics if you prefer to start there.

DANCE

Dancing can be a wonderful and joyful form of self-care and self-expression. Dancing is FUN, and when life gets tough, having fun is essential. I started ballet when I was four years old and continued until I was in middle school, so dancing was a big part of my early life. Now I love hip-hop, Zumba, and nearly any form of dance. Not only is dancing something I love to do, it has helped me get out of my head and into my body. Regularly attending dance class has also helped my coordination in my recovery. Because I move my body in every direction when I dance—forward, backward, sideways, twists and spins, arms and legs doing different things—this is great for the brain and the body. The best part is that dancing can improve balance and coordination without you thinking much of it, since you're just moving to the beat and having fun. You don't have to be considered good at dancing or be able to follow a beat to make it a part of your self-care. You just need to move your body in a way that expresses whatever you want to express, whether to songs on the radio or the song in your head. Solo dance parties happen often in my living room. I just put on my favorite tunes and let myself go. I invite you to do the same.

COLORING

Coloring isn't just for kids anymore. Walk through office supply and even warehouse stores and you'll find coloring books for adults. Themes vary as much as kids' coloring books, but with different topics from those you'll find in the kids' aisle, from swear words to mandalas. Sitting down to color can relieve stress, help you concentrate and exercise parts of your brain that may have deficits resulting from your injuries. Coloring is a fun, creative way to work your brain. For me, thanks to working with my functional neurologist and neuropsychologist, I know that parts of my right hemisphere have some deficits. To exercise this part of my brain, I purposefully spend time coloring with my left hand, because the right half of the brain controls the left side of the body. The right hemisphere of the brain also performs tasks that have to do with creativity, so it gets really worked when I color with my left hand.

Forget about staying between the lines or using realistic colors for a tree, cat, or flower. Even if art has never been your forte or your thing, give it a try, especially when you're stressed or need a break from interacting with the world.

BRAIN GAMES

Playing online brain games, like those on Lumosity.com can help you with attention, memory, focus, reaction time and more. Not only can the games help you with practical, daily necessities, like remembering people's names or a shopping list, they can reveal your strengths and opportunities for improvement in cognitive function. Plus, the games are fun and challenging. In the first year following my TBI, playing these brain games almost daily, and often using them in my treatment with my functional neurologist, helped a lot, and it was fun to see areas of improvement. Being a recovering perfectionist, as I call myself, it was initially difficult to acknowledge tasks and games at which I sucked. When my neurologist reminded me that these tasks are designed to make me fail so that I continually learn and grow, I was able to take off the unnecessary pressure I had placed upon myself. I could even laugh at myself when I did really poorly on a game. Brain games, like those found on Lumosity, come from many of the tests and challenges neuropsychologists use in their assessments, so there is a lot of science and purpose behind these games. Other brain teasers like Sudoku, crossword puzzles, etc. can also be enjoyable self-care and essentially, self-treatment.

Remember, your version of self-care may look different from mine and from anyone else's you know. It should. Hence the use of the word self in self-care. Just as in determining where to start with professional treatment, choose forms of self-care that interest and excite you the most so that you actually do them. Since many TBI survivors get distracted easily and have difficulty with memory and focus, you might find it helpful to put self-care on your daily and weekly calendar, whether that's written down on a paper calendar or the one on your mobile phone. If self-care is on your calendar on your phone, you can set reminders to help you stay consistent. Consistency in both your self-care and professional therapies or treatments is essential to moving forward in your healing process.

Though your form(s) of self-care may change depending on the day and circumstances at hand, make self-care non-negotiable. Often, and I see this especially in women, self-care gets placed at the bottom of the priority list. Kids, work, family and other obligations tend to move up on the list, while self-care keeps getting shoved down to the bottom. One of the greatest and most important lessons my healing journey has taught me is the importance of self-care. I was already good about taking care of myself prior to my TBI, and since my injuries I do not let anything, not even running my own business, stand in the way of implementing some form of self-care every day out of absolute necessity. I could not function or wear the many hats I wear if I didn't. This requires setting firm, yet adaptable boundaries, including saying no to people or things that drain your energy, aren't essential or desired. You may let your partner or family know that your meditation or Lumosity time is from 7:00-7:30 p.m. every night, for example, and that you are not to be disturbed during that time. Granted, sometimes things come up, so adaptability allows you to shift around your self-care, but never takes it off your to-do list. Perhaps you have a parent-teacher conference at your child's school and the only time available is 7:00 p.m. This doesn't mean you don't do your meditation or Lumosity as scheduled, it just means you shift it to a different time that day. If for some reason you get off track, avoid beating yourself up. Just get back on track and keep moving forward. It's not about perfection, but it is about consistency.

Nutrition and Your Other Brain

Healing and living your best life with a TBI requires both outside-in and inside-out approaches. This means that you must get help from outside sources for healing, as well as from within, both the thoughts in your head, and what you put into your body. Food and nutrition are as essential to your brain health as your overall health. In recent decades, scientists and society alike have taken up interest in the relationship between our guts and our brains, called the "Gut-Brain-Axis."[30] The details of this connection are very complex, and more than I am able to share here. For the sake of simplicity, understand that your gut and its colony of bacteria, called the microbiota, act as another "brain." Your microbiota relays important information back to your body and brain that influence memory, mood/emotions, behavior and the process of making decisions.

Depression is a very common repercussion of TBI. When most people think of causes and treatments for depression, the neurotransmitter serotonin is usually the top consideration. While the medical community still doesn't know exactly how much serotonin deficiency is involved with clinical depression, it seems to be an important variable. Serotonin helps regulate sleep, memory, social behavior, appetite, sexual desire and mood. Treatment for depression can include an antidepressant, many of which are selective serotonin uptake inhibitors, or SSRIs. An SSRI decreases your body's resorption of serotonin, making it more available for you to use for regulation of all the things mentioned above. Did you know that approximately 90% of serotonin is made in your gut, and only 10% is made in your brain?[31,32] Surprised? I was, too, when I first learned this.

The good bacteria in your gut, the microbiota (sometimes called the microbiome), produce serotonin. Serotonin gets utilized within the gut itself, as well as circulated into your blood stream and transmitted to your brain cells. Therefore, if you want more naturally-occurring serotonin available to your brain to help boost your mood, memory, libido, appetite and sleep, then you must develop a healthy gut.

Because of the overuse of antibiotics and modern diets high in processed, food-like products, most people's microbiota is unhealthy. Thankfully, there are simple things you can do and eat to help ensure that your good gut bacteria flourishes along with your physical and emotional health.

Start supporting your gut health by taking a good quality probiotic supplement. Probiotics contain billions of strains of these good bacteria, replenishing the population of your microbiota. Not all probiotic supplements are created equal, however, so be sure to consult a nutrition professional before selecting an over-the-counter probiotic. You can also eat or drink probiotics in fermented foods like kimchi, sauerkraut, plain yogurt, kefir, and kombucha. These fermented foods are found in most health food stores, and you can also make them yourself.

These good bacteria in your gut also need food. Certain foods act as what are called prebiotics to the probiotics, meaning, food for these little guys. Prebiotic foods you can eat that feed your good gut bacteria include:[33]

- Garlic
- Onions
- Bananas
- Sunchokes/Jerusalem Artichokes
- Dandelion greens
- Asparagus
- Leeks
- Cocoa
- Oats
- Apples

A healthy gut microbiota can only help ensure a healthier brain and body, making you a happier person. If you aren't familiar with some of the foods mentioned above, or don't know how to prepare them, search online for recipes and try one you've never had before. Add them to a diet filled with a variety of fruits and vegetables, preferably locally-sourced and organic, and you are on your way to improving your mood, memory, sleep, concentration, libido and overall health.

Get started now, by writing down one way you are going to support your gut health below:

_____

_____

_____

SUPPLEMENTS

Though I am a firm believer in obtaining as much nutrition from whole foods as possible, in our modern world, lifestyles and diets, it's not always possible to get enough essential nutrients from food alone. This is especially true when needing to support the brain after a TBI. Any physical injury results in inflammation. Chronic inflammation in the brain and body deteriorates your immune system, and certain supplements effectively act as anti-inflammatories and antioxidants. Antioxidants reduce the amount of damage caused by chronic inflammation, which results from free radical activity. Free radicals are unpaired metabolic electrons which are generated by pollutants and chemicals in the environment, excessive stress, radiation from the sun and other sources, inflammatory foods, poor detoxification and more.

In my own healing process, I've used nutrition to support my brain and overall health. You may consider working with a naturopathic physician (ND), dietician (RD), nutritionist, clinical nutritional consultant (CNC), or other health professional to guide you in which supplements are right for you. Working with a trusted professional to select supplements will help ensure the best rate of return on your investment, and the best for your health. Not all supplements are created equal, and in my personal experience with them, you get what you pay for. Plus, certain nutrients must be combined with others for maximum absorption and utilization by your body. Taking supplements blindly is not likely going to give you the results you're seeking. Your nutrition professional will lead you in the right direction.

Here are just some of the nutrients I've included in my supplement regimen that have proved helpful as part of my nutritional support protocol. Some are blended with others in specific formulas, and some I take individually. Always check with your health professional before starting any supplement to ensure that there are no contraindications, concerns, or potential interactions with any medications you may be taking.

L-TRYPTOPHAN

L-Tryptophan is an essential amino acid. You may have heard of it in relation to the feelings of relaxation and tiredness after eating turkey at Thanksgiving dinner, but it does much more than that. Tryptophan gets converted into the neurotransmitter serotonin, which regulates sleep, appetite, libido, bowel function, bone density, and mood. It's also essential for the formation of vitamin B3 (niacin), which aids the function of the nervous system, circulation, skin, digestion and enhances memory.

If you have trouble sleeping, have migraines, or anxiety, tryptophan may be helpful for improving your symptoms.

Food sources of tryptophan include meat, brown rice, peanuts, cottage cheese and soy protein.

5-HTP

If you experience chronic insomnia resulting from depression, anxiety, headaches or other TBI-related challenges, then 5-hydroxytryptophan (5-HTP) might help. Tryptophan gets converted to 5-HTP before its final conversion into serotonin. By taking supplemental 5-HTP, your body has one less step to take before converting and producing more serotonin.

ALPHA-LIPOIC ACID (ALA)

Alpha-lipoid acid is an antioxidant, which also stimulates the production and absorption of other antioxidants. ALA protects nerve tissue from oxidative stress, reduces cholesterol, detoxifies the liver of metals and controls blood sugar. Cells need ALA to convert sugar into energy.

Food sources of ALA include broccoli, spinach, potatoes, organ meats and brewer's yeast.

ACETYL-L-CARNITINE

Generally considered an amino acid, acetyl-L-carnitine is used by the mitochondria of cells to produce energy. This energy fuels muscles, so this supplement may help with fatigue. It is used to treat cognitive disorders, depression and even Alzheimer's, because of its protective effect on the brain and nervous system.

Food sources of this nutrient come only from animal protein.

BACOPA

Bacopa, also known as water hyssop, has been used in Indian traditional medicine, Ayurveda, for millennia. This plant has been proven to increase memory and cognition, particularly in retaining new information. It also proves to reduce depression and anxiety symptoms.[34,35] Bacopa also has antioxidant properties in the brain, offering protection from free radical damage caused by the environment, food and other sources of free radicals.

GAMMA-AMINOBUTYRIC ACID (GABA)

GABA is an amino acid that acts like a neurotransmitter in the brain, which means that it helps nerves communicate. When taken in the appropriate dose, GABA reduces anxiety and stress, naturally calming and relaxing the body.

Fermented foods are the only dietary source of GABA. This includes kefir, yogurt, miso, tempeh, kombucha, sauerkraut and yogurt. Pu-Erh tea also contains GABA.

Foods containing flavonoids that may influence GABA function include berries, citrus fruits, apples, pears, tea, cocoa and wine.

GINKGO BILOBA

Ginkgo has powerful antioxidant effects on the brain and increases circulation—all good things for healing from brain trauma. If you take a blood thinner or pain medication, be sure to consult your physician before taking ginkgo. Ginkgo seeds can be eaten and are included some Asian cuisine, though consumption of seeds can be toxic or fatal. Taking a good quality ginkgo biloba supplement at the dose recommended by a qualified health professional is a better, safer option.

BIOFLAVONOIDS

Bioflavonoids occur in deeply colored fruits and vegetables and are also bioavailable (easily absorbed and utilized) in several excellent supplements. The pigment in these compounds is among the most powerful neutralizers of the free radicals that create inflammation. This is so important in considering the treatment of TBI because chronic inflammation continually exacerbates TBI symptoms.

There are certainly other supplements that could likely help you, based on your individual challenges and needs. When you begin to think of food as medicine, it changes your perspective on what you are or are not putting into your body. When I worked with a CNC and my physician (who has extensive knowledge in nutraceuticals, aka supplements), I noticed a lot of positive changes. My energy and memory improved, I slept better, and I was even able to replace my anti-depressant with a supplement. Sometimes supplements are as good as or better than pharmaceuticals, or at least can support any drugs that you are taking. Remember that even holistic remedies can have side effects or cautions, so do consult with a professional before you begin adding supplements into your regimen.

In my journey of healing and living with a TBI, I have found specific supplement brands, in particular, that have offered an appreciable improvement in my health and healing. You are welcome to contact me via the contact form my website, www.headofhope.com, if you would like recommendations about the supplement brands I have found to be most effective in my own treatment.

Mindset Matters

As I've said before, recovering from and living with a traumatic brain injury and its subsequent challenges is often long, challenging and lonely. You might get frustrated when other people just don't "get it," you don't know who to see or what to do and have to try to navigate life with a new normal. Your mindset, or how you think, can keep you stuck or help you move forward in both your healing process and in life. While I am a strong believer in the power of the mind and positive thinking, I am also very real and acknowledge that some days things just suck.

IT'S OKAY NOT TO BE OKAY—SOMETIMES.

In the early months and even into the first couple of years following my injuries, I put every ounce of effort into being "okay" so that no one could tell I was struggling with the mental and emotional challenges, as well as a plummet in my energy. Honestly, I got so good at faking being normal that no one knew that anything was wrong with me unless I took off my metaphorical mask. I do not pretend anymore.

There were days when I really wasn't okay; I was in deep depression and needed a tremendous amount of support. Admittedly, some days have been, and still are, better than others. For years I experienced a roller coaster. I would feel good for a day, but then crash, exhausted and very depressed the next. Learning to take it one day at a time has been essential to my healing journey and will be for yours, too. I learned to be okay with cancelling get-togethers, meetings, etc. to take care of myself. The challenging part was not feeling guilty about it. The more I practiced self-care with firm boundaries, the easier it became not to feel guilty. After all, I did nothing wrong by taking care of myself in an act of stewardship and responsibility that not only served me, but those around me. Therefore, I had nothing about which to truly feel guilty. Get used to disappointing others and saying no to people or things when you need to. In the long-run it will serve you far better than pushing through and pretending that you're your pre-TBI Self. These boundaries might even show you who are and are not your best supporters.

If and when you're ready, start to open up to friends, family, and anyone else who is worthy of knowing your story. I say "worthy" because some people will not care or won't be willing or able to support you in the ways you need, even if that's just a listening ear. Be mindful with whom you share your story, your challenges, and needs. Some people also just don't need to know. When I began to open up to my friends, family and even my clients, it was incredibly liberating. Let's get real, open and honest with what *is* right now, without judgement or creating a label of good or bad. Allow your feelings as they are and seek guidance from someone you trust, like your counselor, if you need help processing them.

You may have experienced or experience days where it feels like the world is ending. In reality, you're still here: breathing and living. The world has not ended. There were times when my insomnia was so bad that I did not want to keep on living. Sleep deprivation is torture, especially when it's nightly for months at a time. I was, in my perception, <u>not</u> okay. People know me as a generally happy and positive person, so for me to have passive suicidal ideation (meaning with no intent for action) scared the shit out of me and my husband when I told him. With the help of my counselor, I realized that I really was okay. My world was not ending. My counselor helped me see the blessings in my life amidst my immediate suffering, while not discrediting my experience. I learned that it is truly okay to fall apart, to have dark thoughts, to ask for help, and to not be happy or positive all the time. I had to give myself permission to experience these things without judgment or criticism that there was something wrong with me. It's okay to have those moments when you do not feel okay, so long as you take a step back from the proverbial tree in front of you and see the beauty of the forest that is your life. This doesn't mean pretending that everything is perfect or discrediting your reality. It means staying present with your reality while looking beyond it to see the bigger picture.

You do not have to be strong all the time. You don't have to go this road alone, nor should you. It's not only okay, it's *critical*, to ask for help. It's okay to be angry, frustrated, depressed, or any other emotion you feel so long as you do not get stuck in that mindset. Talk to a counselor or trusted friend to help you gain perspective. Discharge these feelings by going for a run or screaming while beating a pillow with your fists. You can even beat your mattress with a tennis racquet or baseball bat. You *must* discharge that energy and those feelings through your physical body with movement, and not just by talking about them. My personal favorite is to take an object that is broken or that I no longer need and beat it to smithereens with a baseball bat in our garage, all while yelling and screaming. I feel so much better when I'm done, with indiscernible pieces all over the garage floor.

How will you discharge the emotions that aren't serving you? Write it down here:

_____

_____

_____

Remember, take it one day at a time. It's okay not to be okay from time to time but know that you really *are* okay in the bigger picture of your life, even if you haven't yet figured out the details. If you find it exceptionally difficult to be positive, if you have suicidal thoughts or just seem to be stuck in a funk, please reach out to your doctor, counselor or the National Suicide Hotline (in the U.S.) at 1.800.273.8255. Remember that depression and PTSD are very common after a TBI, and you may need both emotional and chemical support through supplements and/or pharmaceuticals to help you shift your mindset. We'll explore how to shift your mindset next.

TRANSFORMING MINDSET

How do you change your mindset from anger, depression or sadness to gratitude, hope and joy? I often turn to books with positive affirmations, opening to a random page each day for something inspiring. I even have a daily tear-off calendar with positive sayings for each day. There are also uplifting cards from the late Dr. Wayne W. Dyer and Louise Hay, respectively, with affirmations you can read daily. Most importantly, practice gratitude every day, particularly when you first get up out of bed. Even on days when you, at first thought, can't think of anything for which to be grateful, take a few minutes to find at least three things for which you are grateful. They do not have to be huge. The little things we so often take for granted are a great place to start. Somedays in my gratitude journal I write: indoor plumbing, our dishwasher, and my favorite blanket. Other days I write down that I am grateful for all the inner work I've done, my healthcare team, and the supplements and pharmaceuticals that help support my health and well-being. Even on the most challenging days, finding gratitude even for a few things at the very beginning of your day will help transform your mindset and your day. Keep a gratitude journal so you can keep track of these things, and even look back at it in the future to see how far you've come.

No matter how challenging your own circumstances, remember this: No one can fix you because you are not broken. You have challenges, but your body, including your brain, are *always* doing the best they can with what is available in the moment. For this we can always be grateful. Your brain has not betrayed or failed you. It is always doing the best it can, even if that is not to the level of your hopes or expectations. Give it time and support, and do the best *you* can do with what you have in any given moment. This is a practice not just for a day, but your entire life.

How will you shift your mindset and find gratitude every single day?

Write down one practice you will implement daily to help keep you positive and grateful:

_____

_____

_____

Letting Go of the Label

Time and time again I see clients, students and people in general create an identity around a condition they have. From sciatica to scoliosis, brain injury to arthritis, people latch on to a diagnosis as if it defines who they are as a person. I hear people say, and have found myself guilty of this as well, "I can't do that because of my [condition]," or they talk about their condition ad nauseam every time you see or speak with them. While limitations and challenges are very real, and we must honor our bodies, it's important to remember that a diagnosis is not You. You are so much more than a brain injury and a TBI survivor. You have skills, talents, gifts, stories, personality, history, ambitions, dreams, goals, and so much more that truly define who you are as a human being. As one of my dear friends battling cancer for a third time recently said to me, "It's just a very small part of my story." Though your TBI may seem a like a HUGE part of your story in the moment, it truly is only a small part of it in the larger story of your life.

As I make videos and write this book, I have had to think a lot about how I want people to know me. Over the past several years, people have heard me talk about my TBI experience a lot, and they talk about it a lot, too, when talking about me. Though my intent with videos, blog posts and this book is to educate and empower other TBI survivors like you, it is ultimately not what I want to be known for in the larger story of my life. I want people to know me for who I am as a person and what I contribute to the world during my life: a wife, sister, daughter, friend, bodyworker, healer, yoga instructor, nutritional consultant, educator, activist, writer, speaker, nature and animal lover, travel enthusiast and all the things I still have yet to do and discover about myself. The TBI is just a small piece of what makes me, Me.

If or when you find yourself clinging to the label of TBI Survivor, depression, anxiety, PTSD, or any other diagnosis you have received, remember the truth of who you are at your heart center. Write down a list of the qualities that make you the person you are, exclusive of anything related to brain injury and post it somewhere you will see if often, like your refrigerator or bathroom mirror. You might write down the things or qualities for which you want to be known or what you value most about yourself.

Let's be real and acknowledge that brain injuries have the capacity to drastically alter people's lives, their ability to function and even their personalities. Each person's injuries impact them differently. It is my own belief that even someone with severe brain trauma never loses the truth of who they are, though their circumstances might change tremendously.

After the third anniversary of my TBI, I held a TBI party, changing the acronym to stand for Totally Blessed Individuals. After a little presentation I gave about brain injuries, my guests began asking questions. One person asked, "How are you different?" I thought about it and first replied with a list of things around memory, energy level, sleep, etc. Then I thought a little more and replied, "I feel like I'm more my Self now than I was before." I meant it and still mean it today. This healing journey has taught me more about the essence of who I am as a person than anything I've experienced to date. I will not go back to living as the old, pre-TBI Me because that is neither who I am today nor who I will be tomorrow or ten years from now. Rather, I acknowledge the things I have been through, both challenges and accomplishments, and use them to continue growing. Letting go of the past, realizing the present, and being open to the future are key to this and any healing process.

List three things for which you want to be known that have nothing to do with your brain injury:

1.

2.

3.

Discovering the Gift

Whether you realize it and are open to it yet or not, there is a gift in your brain injury. This may be difficult to believe, given what you and I have been through so far. For a long time after my TBI, if someone would have told me there was a gift in my situation, I would have given them an evil look accompanied by a slew of expletives in my head. Once I got through the worst of days, and a coach shared this idea that there was a gift in my TBI, I finally opened myself up to it.

What if you reframed your TBI experience from thinking that it happened *to* you to, instead, that it happened *for* you? How would that change your view and mindset of your TBI story? This idea gave me a completely new perspective and perhaps it will do the same for you.

Can you be, as my friend Brenda says, "willing to be willing" to see the gift of this TBI in your life? This willingness is the first step to discovering your gift, understanding that the gift may not present itself right away. Your gift could take months, years or longer to reveal itself. I believe each person's gift presents itself at the right time, which is out of our control.

Discover your gift(s) by pondering the following questions. Write down your responses so you can see what you've gained from your experience. You may not have answers to all of them yet, and that is perfectly fine. Come back to any unanswered questions at another time.

1. Are you willing to be willing to discover a gift or gifts in living with your TBI?
Circle: Yes No

2. What meaningful lesson(s) have you learned from your experience?

_____

_____

_____

3. Whom have you met because of your TBI who is a blessing to you?

_____

_____

_____

4. Have you ended relationships or stopped doing certain things that no longer serve you because of your TBI?

_____

_____

_____

5. Could your experience help other people in some way? If so, how?

_____

_____

_____

Every TBI survivor's story is unique. My gifts may not be the same as yours or anyone else's. The gifts I've discovered include:

- Sharing my story through writing, videos and speaking to provide resources, validation, empathy and hope for TBI survivors
- Understanding trauma and healing more than ever, making me a better practitioner and more relatable to my clients and students
- The relationships I've built with people and animals
- Discovering the inner strength and purpose I didn't know I had

These are just some of the gifts I've discovered so far, and I know more will continue to reveal themselves, as they will for you, too. My gifts didn't present themselves until years after my TBI. More likely, I wasn't willing to even begin looking for them. I hope you allow yourself the willingness to discover the gifts of your own experience when the time is right, and never give up on following your passion, dreams and purpose.

Life with a brain injury doesn't stop; it changes. It changes in many aspects for the better if you allow, seek and work for it. I hope this book empowers you to be your own advocate in your healing process, and to seek ways and people that can help you move forward and be happy. If nothing else, may this book and my story leave you with a head of hope.

PART III

Epilogue

Recovering from and living with a brain injury has been and continues to be one of my greatest teachers. It has taught me more than I ever wanted to know thus far on the subjects of brain physiology, hormones, psychology, nutrition, strength, acceptance, resilience, determination, purpose, self-discovery, self-care, love, support and compassion. Many of the lessons are lifelong practices that never end and can be applied to oneself and any life situation. It's my own opinion and belief that there was no other way for me to learn the lessons I've needed to learn. Sometimes life must knock you upside the head to get the message across, and that's how I choose to see my own journey.

There are days when I am angry or frustrated at the whole situation and the challenges that are still my daily reality. I allow and release these feelings, continue to take action, get support, and remind myself how far I've come as a person because of this experience. Not knowing if or when I'll continue to see improvement used to scare me, and now I approach the future with curiosity and ask myself, "What's possible?" This applies not just to my brain and health, but rather to my whole life ahead. Living with a TBI has changed my life forever, yet it neither defines who I am nor the things of which I'm capable of achieving. There is so much more to me and my life than my injuries and limitations. That's how I want to be known: for all the other things I am and do in my life, not just as a TBI survivor.

My job here is not done, though. Our society still thinks that concussions aren't a big deal and that they only happen to athletes. There are too many people incurring TBIs and not getting the care and support they need and deserve. There are too few people talking about the long-term ramifications and treatment options. There are too many TBI survivors struggling. Until these things shift, I will continue to advocate and educate so that no other TBI survivor must endure the painful journey I and so many others have gone through. The one thing every person needs to heal is hope. I pray that you've gotten at least a little bit of it from this book and will spread that hope to another who needs it. Together, as a community of survivors and those who care about them, we can uplift and support one another to live our best lives.

Heartfelt Thanks and Gratitude

My sincerest, deepest, heartfelt thanks, gratitude and love to all of those who have supported me in my healing journey and in writing this book. First, to my Love, my husband, Dylan. You have been my rock and I could not have gotten through this without you by my side. Your endless love, support and ability to make me laugh are more precious than gold. I love you and am so grateful to have you in my life.

Thank you to my moms, Nancy and Kerry, for your support and always lending an ear when I needed to talk and cry.

To my healthcare team and the people who referred me to you, thank you. I would not be doing as well as I am today without your compassionate care. My gratitude goes to my colleague, friend and CranioSacral practitioner, Nancy Witt, who passed away before this book's completion. She will always be remembered for her immediate care and influence on this journey.

I am blessed to have the best friends I could possibly imagine, too many to name here. To every one of you who listened, advised, laughed, cried and are still on this journey with me, thank you.

Thank you to my clients and students for trusting and allowing me to guide you in your own healing process. Even on my worst days, my work with you gives me purpose and fills my soul.

Thank you to the animals who have been some of the greatest comforts and teachers in this process: Little League, Columbo, Sasha, Sarah and Dublin. You mean more to me than you or the world will ever know. I love you.

Thank you to my attorney, A.B., who fought for me and won my legal case. It was not an easy task, and I am so thankful for you and your hard work to ensure justice and fair compensation.

Thank you to the many people who contributed to this book: Karin, Tracey, Kathleen, Dan, Barbara, Connie and Drs. Babcox, Burns and Howard. Thank you to my peers who provided feedback: Barb, Susan and Beáta. Thank you to my editor, Catherine, and my proof reader, Jenni. Thank you to my GoFundMe supporters for helping make this book a reality. Thank you to all my friends, family and clients for your encouragement and support. This book wouldn't exist without each and every one of you.

Last, but certainly not least, thank you to Karen Lynn Maher of LegacyOne Authors, who guided me through the publishing process and helped make this vision a reality.

REFERENCES

1. Brain Injury Association of America. http://www.biausa.olr/mild-brain-injury.htm#definition

2. Centers for Disease Control and Prevention. https://www.cdc.gov/traumaticbraininjury/basics.html

3. Gail L. Denton PhD. *Brainlash: Maximize Your Recovery from Mild Brain Injury 3rd Edition.* New York, NY: Demos Health, 2008.

4. Brain Injury Association of America - https://www.biausa.org/brain-injury/about-brain-injury/nbiic/what-is-the-difference-between-an-acquired-brain-injury-and-a-traumatic-brain-injury

5. Jesse R. Fann, Tessa Hart, and Katherine G. Schomer, "Treatment for Depression after Traumatic Brain Injury: A Systematic Review," *Journel of Neurotrauma, no. 12 (2009), doi:* 10.1089/neu.2009.1091, https://www.ncbi.nlm.nih.gov/pmc/articles/PMC2864457/

6. Denise Mann, "More often than not, brain injuries lead to depression," *Health.com,* http://www.cnn.com/2010/HEALTH/05/18/brain.injury.depression/index.html

7. Christopher A. Taylor, PhD; Jeneita M. Bell, MD, MPH; Matthew J. Breiding, PhD; Likang Xu, MD, "Traumatic Brain Injury–Related Emergency Department Visits, Hospitalizations, and Deaths — United States, 2007 and 2013," *Morbidity and Mortality Weekly Report (MMWR),* Surveillance Summaries 2017;66(No. 9):1–16. doi: http://dx.doi.org/10.15585/mmwr.ss6609a1

8. United States Census Bureau. https://www.census.gov/popclock/

9. National Cancer Institute at the National Institutes of Health. https://www.cancer.gov/about-cancer/understanding/statistics

10. Lumosity.com

11. Woolf PD, Lee LA, Hamill RW, McDonald JV, "Thyroid test abnormalities in traumatic brain injury: correlation with neurologic impairment and sympathetic nervous system activation," National Library of Medicine National Institutes of Health, *Pub Med.gov,* https://www.ncbi.nlm.nih.gov/pubmed/3407649

12. Marta Bondanelli, Maria Rosaria Ambrosio, Maria Chiara Zatelli, Laura De Marinis and Ettore C degli Uberti, "Hypopituitarism after traumatic brain injury," *European Journal of Endocrinology, No. 152, (2005), 679-691,* DOI: 10.1530/eje.1.01895, http://www.eje-online.org/content/152/5/679.full

13. Naomi Parker, "Traumatic Brain Injury: a cause of hypothyroidism,"(20016), *National Academy of Hypothyroidism(NAHIS),* https://www.nahypothyroidism.org/traumatic-brain-injury-a-cause-of-hypothyroidism/

14. Vanessa Raymont, Andres M. Salazar, Frank Krueger, Jordan Grafman, "Studying Injured Minds—The Vietnam Head Injury Study and 40 Years of Brain Injury Research," *Front Neurol (2011), 2:15. Doi:10.3389/fneur.2011.00015,* https://www.ncbi.nlm.nih.gov/pmc/articles/PMC3093742/

15. Brain Injury Association Kansas, *CTE and PCS Fact Sheet,* http://www.biausa.org/concussion/cte-pcs-fact-sheet.pdf

16. "What is PCS," Concussion Legacy Foundation, *PCS Resources,* https://concussionfoundation.org/PCS-resources/what-is-PCS

17. What is Sleep Hygiene?" National Sleep Foundation, https://sleepfoundation.org/sleep-topics/sleep-hygiene

18. "Your Hormones," The Pituitary Foundation, *Information: hormones,* https://www.pituitary.org.uk/information/hormones/

19. "Adrenal Insufficiency and Addison's Disease: What is adrenal insufficiency," National Institute of Diabetes and Digestive and Kidney Diseases (NIH), *Health Information,* https://www.niddk.nih.gov/health-information/endocrine-diseases/adrenal-insufficiency-addisons-disease

20. American Psychological Association, *Clinical Neuropsychology 210*, http://www.apa.org/ed/graduate/specialize/neuro.aspx

21. Ricardo E. Jorge, MD; Robert G. Robinson, MD; David Moser, PhD, "Major Depression Following Traumatic Brain Injury," *Jama Psychiatry (2004), 61 (1): 42-50, doi:10.1001/archpsy.61.1.42,* http://jamanetwork.com/journals/jamapsychiatry/fullarticle/481944

22. Jonathan M. Silver , M.D. Thomas W. McAllister , M.D. David B. Arciniegas , M.D., "Depression and Cognitive Complaints Following Mid Traumatic Brain Injury," *The American Journal of Psychiatry, (2009), 166 (6): 653-661,* http://ajp.psychiatryonline.org/doi/full/10.1176/appi.ajp.2009.08111676

23. "What is NIS," NEUROLINK®, http://www.neurolinkglobal.com/what-is-nis/

24. "Muscle Testing," NEUROLINK®, http://www.neurolinkglobal.com/what-is-nis/how-does-nis-work/muscle-testing/

25. "What is EMDR," EMDR Institute, Inc. Eye Movement Desensitization and Reprocessing, http://www.emdr.com/what-is-emdr/

26. "Frequently Asked Questions About CranioSacral Therapy, Upledger Institute International, *CST Facts,* https://www.upledger.com/therapies/faq.php

27. "Why Choose Chiropractic," American Chiropractic Association, *Patients,* https://www.acatoday.org/Patients/Why-Choose-Chiropractic/What-is-Chiropractic

28. International Association of Structural Integrators (IASI),"New to Structural Integration," *Certification Board from Structural Integration,* http://www.theiasi.net/what-is-structural-integration-

29. "About the Medicine," National Certification Commission for Acupuncture and Oriental Medicine (NCCAOM), http://www.nccaom.org/about-the-medicine/

30. Augusto J. Montiel-Castro, Rina M. González-Cervantes, Gabriela Bravo-Ruiseco and Gustavo Pacheco-López, "The microbiota-gut-brain axis: neurobehavioral correlates, health and sociality," *Frontiers in Integrative Neuroscience, (2013), 7:70, doi: 10.3389/fnint.2013.00070,* https://www.ncbi.nlm.nih.gov/pmc/articles/PMC3791857/

31. Jessica Stoller-Conrad, "Microbes Help Produce Serotonin in Gut," *Caltech (2015)*, http://www.caltech.edu/news/microbes-help-produce-serotonin-gut-46495

32. Kristina Campbell, "Know your serotonin: An interview with gut-brain axis researcher Elaine Hsiaso," *Get Microbiota News Watch, (2017)*, http://www.gutmicrobiotaforhealth.com/en/know-serotonin-interview-gut-brain-axis-researcher-elaine-hsiao/

33. "The 19 Best Prebiotic Foods You Should Eat," *Healthline*, https://www.healthline.com/nutrition/19-best-prebiotic-foods

34. Carlo Calabrese, N.D., M.P.H., William L. Gregory, Ph.D., Michael Leo, Ph.D., Dale Kraemer, Ph.D., Kerry Bone, F.N.I.M.H., F.N.H.A.A., and Barry Oken, M.D., "Effects of a Standardized *Bacopa monnieri* Extract on Cognitive Performance, Anxiety, and Depression in the Elderly: A Randomized, Double-Blind Placebo-Controlled Trial," US National Library of Medicine National Institutes of Health, *Journal of Alternative and Complementary Medicine,(2008), doi:10,1089/acm 2008 0018*, https://www.ncbi.nlm.nih.gov/pmc/articles/PMC3153866/

35. Sebastian Aguiar and Thomas Borowski, "Neuropharmacological Review of the Nootropic Herb *Bacopa Monnieri*," US National Library of Medicine National Institutes of Health *(2013) 4, 313-326, doi:10.1089/rej. 2013.1431*, https://www.ncbi.nlm.nih.gov/pmc/articles/PMC3746283/

ABOUT THE AUTHOR

Jennifer Soames is a TBI survivor, board certified Structural Integrator (BCSI), certified yoga instructor, and nutritional consultant. She is passionate about helping other TBI survivors get the information, care and support they need to live their best life. Outside of her professional practice and writing, Jennifer enjoys spending time in nature, hiking, and camping. She also enjoys practicing yoga, weight training, traveling and spending time with her husband, family, friends, and animals. She lives near Seattle, Washington, USA.

Photo credit: Jill Labberton Lifestyle Portraits

Contact Jennifer with though her website at www.headofhope.com or at headofhope@gmail.com.